1,000 AMAZING GROSS FACTS

AUG ' 2023

Senior editors Ben Morgan, Shaila Brown
Senior art editor Vikas Chauhan
Project editor Sarah MacLeod
Editor Caroline Bingham
Art editors Laura Gardner Design Studio,
Samantha Richiardi, Tanvi Sahu,
Heena Sharma, Diya Verma
US editor Heather Wilcox
US executive editor Lori Cates Hand
Assistant picture researcher
Nunhoih Guite
Illustrators Adam Benton, Peter Bull,
Stuart Jackson-Carter, Dynamo Ltd.,
Jon@KJA-artists.com, Arran Lewis, Andrew
Pagram (Beehive Illustration), Gus Scott
Managing editor Rachel Fox

Managing art editors Owen Peyton Jones,
Govind Mittal
DTP Designers Jaypal Chauhan,
Ashok Kumar, Rakesh Kumar
Production editors Gillian Reid, Kavita Varma
Senior production controller
Meskerem Berhane
Jacket designer Akiko Kato
Senior jackets coordinator
Priyanka Sharma Saddi
Jacket design development manager
Sophia MTT
Publisher Andrew Macintyre
Associate publishing director Liz Wheeler
Art director Karen Self
Publishing director Jonathan Metcalf

Written by Stevie Derrick, Andrea Mills, Ben Morgan

Content previously published in *The Science of Goo!* and *It Can't Be True! Poo!*

First American Edition, 2023
Published in the United States by DK Publishing
1745 Broadway, 20th Floor, New York, NY 10019

Copyright © 2023 Dorling Kindersley Limited
DK, a Division of Penguin Random House LLC
23 24 25 26 27 10 9 8 7 6 5 4 3 2
002–334463–June/2023

All rights reserved.
Without limiting the rights under the copyright reserved above, no part
of this publication may be reproduced, stored in or introduced into a retrieval
system, or transmitted, in any form, or by any means (electronic, mechanical,
photocopying, recording, or otherwise), without the prior written permission
of the copyright owner.
Published in Great Britain by Dorling Kindersley Limited.

A catalog record for this book is available from the Library of Congress.
ISBN 978-0-7440-8143-5

DK books are available at special discounts when purchased in bulk for sales
promotions, premiums, fund-raising, or educational use. For details, contact:
DK Publishing Special Markets, 1745 Broadway, 20th Floor, New York, NY 10019
SpecialSales@dk.com

Printed and bound in China

For the curious
www.dk.com

This book was made with Forest
Stewardship Council™ certified
paper—one small step in DK's
commitment to a sustainable future.
**For more information, go to
www.dk.com/our-green-pledge.**

1 ALL ABOUT GOO

2 ALL ABOUT POO

All about goo

Get ready for some seriously sticky situations. From the wonders of nature to the marvels of science, there is a whole world of gooey gunk and slimy stuff to explore…

Male reticulated glass frogs are left on guard duty. The clammy, jelly-covered eggs laid by females under leaves need careful protection. Any enemies that come too close receive a nasty kick!

GIANT
SLIME

From sticky snot and slimy snail trails to stretchy toy slime and giant fatbergs, goo is found just about everywhere. Whether it is **sticky, slimy, slippery, or sludgy,** goo is fascinating stuff.

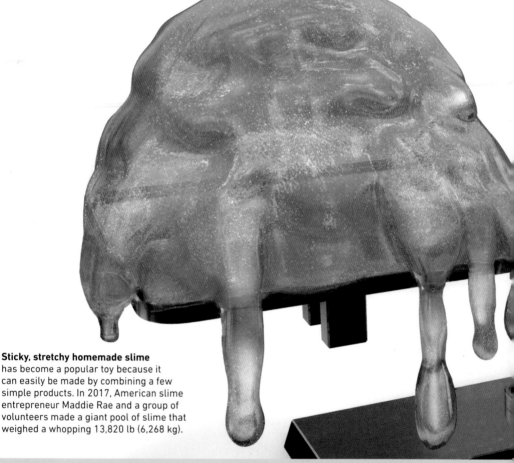

Maddie Rae's giant slime weighed 13,820 lb (6,268 kg)— equal to four hippos.

Sticky, stretchy homemade slime
has become a popular toy because it can easily be made by combining a few simple products. In 2017, American slime entrepreneur Maddie Rae and a group of volunteers made a giant pool of slime that weighed a whopping 13,820 lb (6,268 kg).

AT THE AGE OF 10, CIELA VILLA BROKE A WORLD RECORD FOR STRETCHING HOMEMADE SLIME 7 FT 4 IN (2.25 M).

IN 1968, APOLLO 8 ASTRONAUTS TOOK A TYPE OF SLIME CALLED SILLY PUTTY INTO SPACE.

FAST FACTS

Slime requires three key ingredients:

Contact lens solution can be used as an activator.

Activator (a solution that contains boron)

Water

Craft glue

Craft glue is made up of molecules arranged in long chains that can slide past each other. Adding water helps the molecules slide more easily. When an activator is added, the boron it contains sticks the chains together, turning the mixture into strong, stretchy slime.

Glue and water

+

Activator

Slime

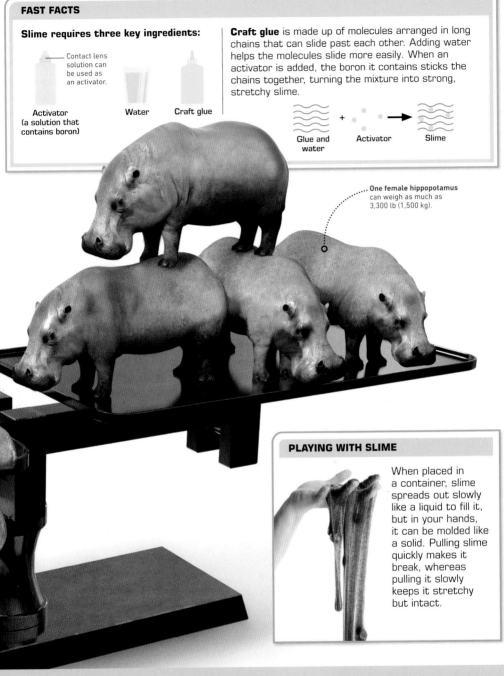

One female hippopotamus can weigh as much as 3,300 lb (1,500 kg).

PLAYING WITH SLIME

When placed in a container, slime spreads out slowly like a liquid to fill it, but in your hands, it can be molded like a solid. Pulling slime quickly makes it break, whereas pulling it slowly keeps it stretchy but intact.

 MONTRÉAL SCIENCE CENTRE HELD THE WORLD'S **LARGEST** SLIME-MAKING LESSON (FOR 491 PEOPLE).

 A NASA ENGINEER BUILT THE TALLEST **SLIME VOLCANO.** IT SHOT GOO 250 FT (76 M) INTO THE AIR.

DEVIL'S FINGERS
FUNGUS

Like fingers sprouting from the ground, these **fiendish fungi** have blood-red tentacles covered in a **dark, foul-smelling goo** that attracts insects.

The fungi are also known as octopus stinkhorns for their tentacle-like fingers.

Native to Australia and now found across Europe and North America, devil's fingers fungi grow from egglike cases in woodland soil to reveal vibrant red fingers. The dark slime on the fingers contains the seedlike spores needed for new fungi to grow and has a strong stench of rotting meat. Flies and other bugs are attracted by the smell, eat the slime, and spread the spores in their droppings.

AFTER THE FINGERS EMERGE, IT TAKES FLIES JUST 48 HOURS TO EAT THE SLIMY SPORES.

A TYPE OF FUNGUS CALLED **BLEEDING TOOTH** OOZES BLOODLIKE RED GOO FROM DEEP PORES.

FAST FACTS

New devil's fingers fungi grow from tiny spores. When they land on the ground, the spores grow threads called hyphae, which fuse with other hyphae, feed on the soil, and develop into new fungi.

An egg-shaped fungus grows from a knot of mycelium.

The fungus fruiting body emerges, and a fly eats its spore-filled slime.

The insect flies away and spreads the spores in its poo.

Hyphae grow into a network called mycelium, in which knots form.

Spores germinate to form hyphae, which fuse with other hyphae.

Sticky slime may be carried on a fly's body as well as in its poo and spread over large distances.

The smelly black goo contains the spores, which will grow into new fungi.

77

DEVIL'S FINGERS BELONGS TO A FUNGUS FAMILY (THE STINKHORNS) OF AROUND 77 SPECIES.

SOME SPECIES OF STINKHORN GROW SO FAST, THEY HAVE ENOUGH **FORCE** TO CRACK PAVEMENT.

SLIPPERY
FROG SPAWN

Female frogs lay their gooey, jellylike eggs, called frog spawn, underwater. Some species can lay as many as **100,000 eggs in their lifetime**.

GLASS FROGS

Named for their transparent appearance, the glass frogs of Central and South America lay their eggs on leaves. Unlike most other species of frogs, the males guard the eggs from predators that try to eat them. Their glassy skin makes them almost impossible to spot.

Tough, transparent jelly surrounds the embryo, providing protection.

A YOUNG **FROGLET** IS SMALL ENOUGH TO FIT ON YOUR FINGERNAIL.

ONE OF THE WORLD'S **SMALLEST** FROGS HATCHES FROM ITS EGG AS A FULLY FORMED MINIATURE FROG.

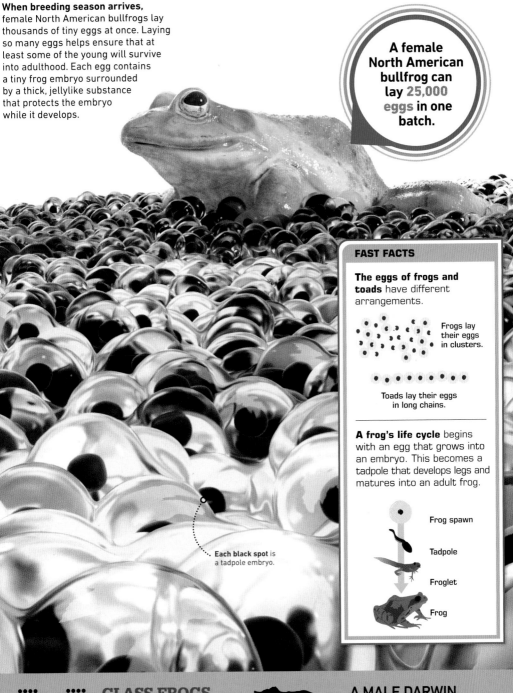

When breeding season arrives, female North American bullfrogs lay thousands of tiny eggs at once. Laying so many eggs helps ensure that at least some of the young will survive into adulthood. Each egg contains a tiny frog embryo surrounded by a thick, jellylike substance that protects the embryo while it develops.

A female North American bullfrog can lay **25,000 eggs** in one batch.

Each black spot is a tadpole embryo.

FAST FACTS

The eggs of frogs and toads have different arrangements.

Frogs lay their eggs in clusters.

Toads lay their eggs in long chains.

A frog's life cycle begins with an egg that grows into an embryo. This becomes a tadpole that develops legs and matures into an adult frog.

Frog spawn

Tadpole

Froglet

Frog

GLASS FROGS MAY LOOK DELICATE, BUT THEY CAN LIVE FOR UP TO **14 YEARS**.

A MALE DARWIN FROG CARRIES EGGS IN HIS **VOCAL SACK**, WHERE THEY HATCH AS TADPOLES.

GLOBULES OF SLIMY
SNOT

Grab a tissue! You constantly make gooey gunk in your nose and throat. In fact, each person produces as much as **3.2 pints (1.5 liters) of slimy snot** every day.

The eruption of Mount Vesuvius in 79 CE produced about 1 cubic mile (4 cubic km) of volcanic ash, mud, and rock.

BIG BLOWHOLE

Whales have huge nostrils, called blowholes, on the tops of their heads. When they surface, whales open their blowholes to breathe and will shoot high plumes made up of water, air, and mucus into the air. When the whales dive back underwater, their blowholes close to keep water from flooding in.

Humans produce **8.9 trillion pints (4.2 trillion liters) of snot** every year.

The snot produced in your nose and throat is really called mucus. Although it may be messy, mucus is essential to survival. It consists mostly of water, but its gooey, sticky consistency protects you by catching any dust, bacteria, and viruses you inhale through your nose. We swallow most of this mucus without noticing.

SNOT IS **MUCUS** FROM OUR NOSE. MUCUS FROM OUR LUNGS IS CALLED PHLEGM.

CILIA (TINY HAIRS) MOVE SNOT OUT OF YOUR NOSE AT .04 IN (1 MM) PER SECOND.

FAST FACTS

A 1995 study found that 91 percent of people pick their nose.

Tears

Tear duct

Runny snot

Not all tears roll down your face when you cry. Some drain through a tiny hole in the corner of the eye and into a channel called the tear duct. This duct drains into your nose, where your tears mix with snot, resulting in a runny nose.

Bacterium

Virus

Cilia

Goblet cell

Mucus is made in your nose and throat by goblet cells, named after their shape. When a cold virus infects the nose, these cells produce more mucus. Inhaled bacteria and viruses become caught in the mucus and are swept away by tiny hairs called cilia to be swallowed.

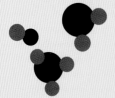

LARGE MOLECULES INSIDE SNOT CALLED MUCINS MAKE ITS TEXTURE SLIPPERY.

MEHMET ÖZYÜREK HAS THE WORLD'S LONGEST KNOWN NOSE, AT 3.55 IN (8.8 CM).

NATURE'S
NOSE PICKERS

Boogers can block the noses of many animals, not only humans, so our furry friends have had to find some interesting ways to **keep the snot at bay**.

Dogs are known for their wet noses, which are covered with watery mucus to keep them cool and enhance their sense of smell. Their long tongues are perfect for licking away any excess snot that drips from their snouts. ▼

◄ **Buffaloes rely on oxpeckers** to peck dust, dirt, and parasites from their bodies, keeping their skin clean and healthy. These small birds have even been spotted using their beaks to feast on the sticky snot of buffaloes.

12 THE STAR-NOSED MOLE USES ITS NOSE LIKE A HAND TO FEEL **12** OBJECTS A SECOND.

AN **ELEPHANT'S TRUNK** IS AN ELONGATED NOSE, MEASURING UP TO 7 FT (2 M) LONG.

As well as long necks, giraffes have long, nimble tongues. This means that they can control the tongue muscles to grab and grasp, making their tongues just right to reach into the nostrils to lick or push away snot. ▶

Clever chimpanzees use tools for all kinds of work, and nose-picking is no exception. They poke sticks carefully up each nostril to clear mucus, dislodge blockages, and even trigger sneezes that clear the airways. Although it may work for chimpanzees, you should not try this yourself! ▼

Giraffes use their 20-in- (50-cm-) long tongues to dig snot from their noses.

When bonobo babies get stuffed up, their mothers pull out all the stops to make them feel better. One female was witnessed helping her offspring breathe more easily by using her own mouth to suck out the gooey snot blocking her newborn's nostrils. ▼

Like many humans, gorillas stick their fingers up their noses to scrape out boogers, before carefully inspecting any snot they find and eating it. ▶

BLACK BEARS CAN SMELL FOOD UP TO 20 MILES (32 KM) AWAY.

PROBOSCIS MONKEYS USE THEIR 4 IN (10 CM) NOSES TO PRODUCE LOUD, HONKING CALLS.

Tokay geckos are often seen inside homes in the tropics as well as in their rainforest habitat.

TONGUE TRICK

Most geckos don't have eyelids, so they use their extra-long tongues to lick their eyes clean. This wipes away any yucky morning dew and dirt. Although geckos may look like harmless little lizards, don't mess with them! These super-speedy sprinters can climb walls, stick to surfaces, grow new tails, and give a painful bite. Ouch!

MARINE MARVEL

The eyes of cuttlefish change shape according to light levels. The pupils take on a unique W-shape in bright light but become round in darkness. Scientists think that cuttlefish adapt their pupils to judge distances with more accuracy, but it may be to keep their eyes camouflaged from predators.

Vitreous humor has a thick consistency in children but deteriorates with age and becomes more runny.

SQUISHY
EYEBALL

Our eyeballs are **fluid-filled organs** that help us see the world. Human eyeballs contain a **thick goo the consistency of egg whites**.

80% of the human eyeball is made up of transparent goo.

THE AVERAGE PERSON BLINKS AROUND 12 TIMES A MINUTE. THAT'S 4,200,000 TIMES A YEAR!

SMALL PRIMATES CALLED **TARSIERS** HAVE THE LARGEST EYES RELATIVE TO BODY SIZE OF ANY MAMMAL.

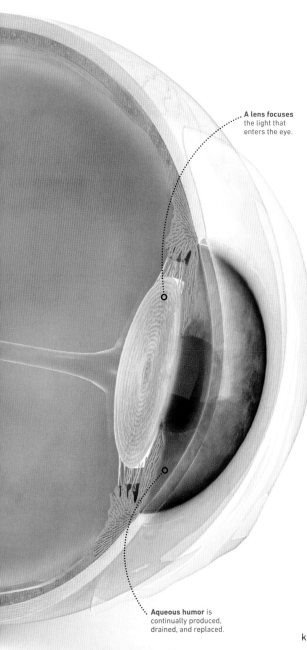

A lens focuses the light that enters the eye.

Aqueous humor is continually produced, drained, and replaced.

FAST FACTS

The colossal squid can reach 39 ft (12 m) long and has the largest eyeballs of any living creature. The eye of one specimen measured 11 in (27 cm) wide—bigger than a basketball. Giant eyes help squid spot predatory whales.

Colossal squid eye   Basketball

Sea stars, or starfish, are basic creatures with no brain. However, most of them have a tiny eye at the tip of each arm. These very simple eyes do not offer clear vision but vague images that help them find their way underwater.

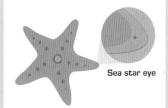

Sea star eye

The human eyeball contains two goo-filled spaces. A small space in front of the lens holds a watery liquid called the aqueous humor, which provides the lens with nutrients. A much larger space behind the lens is filled with thicker, gel-like goo called the vitreous humor. This fluid keeps the eyeball in a round shape, like the air in a football, and acts as a shock absorber.

CHAMELEONS CAN MOVE THEIR EYES INDEPENDENTLY OF EACH OTHER.

GOATS HAVE RECTANGULAR-SHAPED PUPILS THAT ALLOW THEM TO SEE DANGER TO THE SIDE.

HONEYDEW
FARMING

Ants and aphids have a relationship that benefits both sides—**strong ants protect tiny aphids** in return for the **sweet treat** they produce, honeydew.

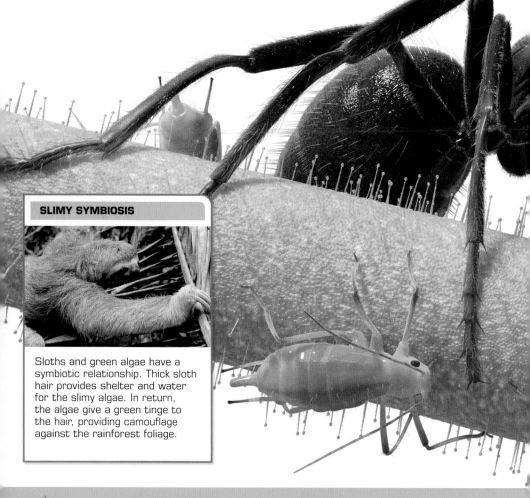

SLIMY SYMBIOSIS

Sloths and green algae have a symbiotic relationship. Thick sloth hair provides shelter and water for the slimy algae. In return, the algae give a green tinge to the hair, providing camouflage against the rainforest foliage.

ONE APHID CAN PRODUCE A FAMILY OF **BILLIONS** IN ONE YEAR.

SOME **FISH SCALE GECKOS** IN MADAGASCAR DRINK HONEYDEW FROM APHIDS.

FAST FACT

Ants will stop at nothing in their mission to keep aphids close by.

Ants have been known to bite off the wings of aphids in order to keep them from flying away.

Chemicals released from the feet of ants leave a trail. The chemicals make the aphids sleepy and slow-moving, so they cannot stray.

Ants will fight off predators, such as ladybugs, that threaten the aphids, making sure their source of honeydew stays safe.

Stroking **the back of aphids** stimulates the release of **honeydew droplets**.

Ants consume the sweet honeydew produced by the aphids.

When aphids eat the sap of plants, they produce sugar-rich honeydew as waste. Hungry ants farm colonies of aphids to feast on this waste. In return, ants use their size and strength to care for the aphids and keep attackers away. This is an example of a symbiotic relationship, which brings benefits to both species.

ONE TYPE OF APHID MIMICS ANT LARVAE. ANTS TAKE IT TO THEIR NEST, AND IT **EATS** THEIR YOUNG.

THE **LARGEST** KNOWN ANTS' NEST WAS MORE THAN 3,700 MILES (5,955 KM) WIDE.

GLOWING
TRAP

Sneaky New Zealand glow worms secrete **sticky strands of goo** from their mouths before lighting up their bright blue glowing tails. Unsuspecting bugs are attracted to this light and quickly find themselves **stuck in the deadly traps**.

A glow worm's sticky silk traps can be as long as 20 in (50 cm).

After hatching inside the Waitomo Caves of New Zealand, these glow worms build tubes of mucus along the cave ceilings and cough up as many as 30 silk threads to hang from them. The glow worms coat these strands with sticky droplets, light their glowing tails, and wait in the darkness for their dinner to arrive.

NEW ZEALAND GLOW WORMS ARE THE LARVAE OF A TYPE OF FLYING INSECT CALLED A FUNGUS GNAT.

THE WAITOMO CAVES IN NEW ZEALAND ARE 30 MILLION YEARS OLD.

FAST FACTS

99% water

1% waste

Glow worm glue is almost entirely water. Just 1 percent is made up of bodily waste—salt, protein, and urea (a chemical found in urine).

Glow worms are not the only creatures in the animal kingdom to produce silk:

Weaver ants build nests by connecting leaves with silk.

Silkworms make silk cocoons for their metamorphoses into moths.

Spiders construct silky webs to trap their prey.

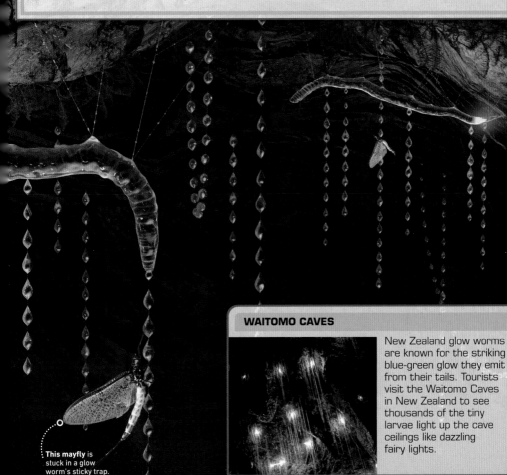

This mayfly is stuck in a glow worm's sticky trap.

WAITOMO CAVES

New Zealand glow worms are known for the striking blue-green glow they emit from their tails. Tourists visit the Waitomo Caves in New Zealand to see thousands of the tiny larvae light up the cave ceilings like dazzling fairy lights.

EACH SILK STRING IS ABOUT ONE-SIXTH THE WIDTH OF A HUMAN HAIR.

IT CAN TAKE A GLOW WORM UP TO 15 MINUTES TO CREATE A SINGLE SILK STRING.

MONSTER
FATBERG

In 2017, a **giant fatberg** was discovered lurking in the sewers of London, UK. The **sticky, congealed mass of waste** gave off a disgusting stench and blocked the sewage system.

The London fatberg was 820 ft (250 m) long and weighed 143 tons (130 metric tons). It was made up of cooking oil and animal fat that had combined with solid substances that should not be flushed down the toilet, such as wet wipes and diapers. This mass of sludge hardened and built up over time to form the giant blockage.

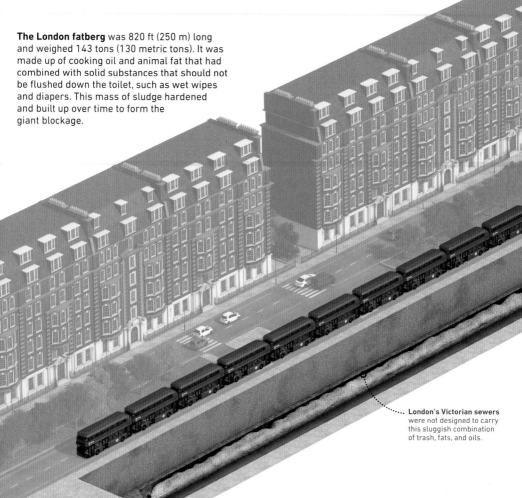

London's Victorian sewers were not designed to carry this sluggish combination of trash, fats, and oils.

STRANGE THINGS HAVE BEEN FOUND IN FATBERGS, INCLUDING FALSE TEETH AND A BOWLING BALL.

A FATBERG FOUND IN ENGLAND IN 2019 WEIGHED ABOUT THE SAME AS **63 ELEPHANTS**.

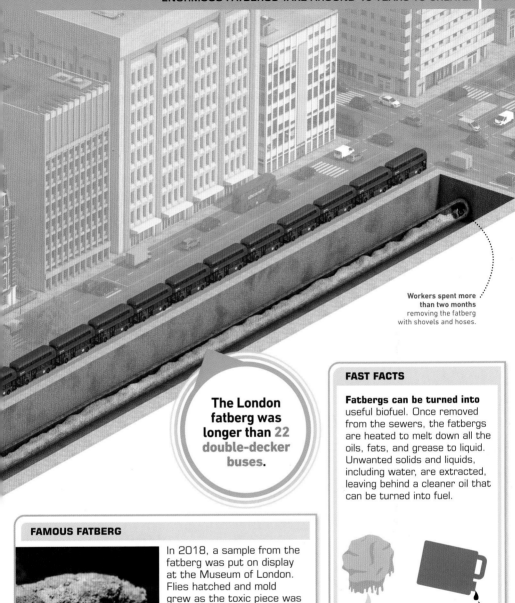

Workers spent more than two months removing the fatberg with shovels and hoses.

The London fatberg was longer than 22 double-decker buses.

FAST FACTS

Fatbergs can be turned into useful biofuel. Once removed from the sewers, the fatbergs are heated to melt down all the oils, fats, and grease to liquid. Unwanted solids and liquids, including water, are extracted, leaving behind a cleaner oil that can be turned into fuel.

FAMOUS FATBERG

In 2018, a sample from the fatberg was put on display at the Museum of London. Flies hatched and mold grew as the toxic piece was prepared for display, and it released the eye-watering stench of a dirty toilet.

2.2 ENGLAND AND WALES PRODUCE **2.2 BILLION GALLONS** (10 BILLION LITERS) OF SEWAGE A DAY.

$ FATBERGS COST US CITIES **BILLIONS** OF DOLLARS A YEAR TO REMOVE.

The **Great Pacific Garbage Patch** covers an area three times the size of France.

PLASTIC POLLUTION

Known as the Great Pacific Garbage Patch, this supersized, swirling mass of trash is littering the Pacific Ocean. The huge expanse of plastic waste floats along on ocean currents, polluting the waters and endangering marine life. Recycling plastic can help keep the garbage patch from getting any bigger.

SUPER
SALIVA

Each person produces 1.1–3.2 pints (**500–1500 ml**) of saliva every day. The **slimy fluid** performs many important functions to keep your mouth healthy and help you digest the food you eat.

In one week, a person makes enough saliva to fill **30 drink cans**.

TAKE AIM AND SPIT

Archerfish will spit mouthfuls of water as far as 6.5 ft (2 m) above a river's surface to catch prey. The powerful jets of water knock insects off leaves and branches into the river for the fish to eat.

SALIVA CONTAINS CHEMICALS THAT FIGHT **BACTERIA**. THAT'S WHY SOME ANIMALS LICK THEIR WOUNDS.

NOT ALL MAMMALS PRODUCE SALIVA. **WHALES** HAVE NO USE FOR SALIVA.

Your mouth is producing saliva constantly. The slippery slime kills bacteria in your mouth and protects your teeth. When you eat, saliva even helps the tongue taste food and gives food a slippery coating that makes swallowing easier. Digestive enzymes in saliva begin the digestion process by starting to break down any food you eat before it travels down to your stomach.

FAST FACTS

Saliva is produced by organs called salivary glands. There are three major salivary glands on each side of your mouth—the parotid gland, the submandibular gland, and the sublingual gland. There are also hundreds of tiny minor salivary glands all around your mouth. All these glands secrete saliva into your mouth through tiny channels called ducts.

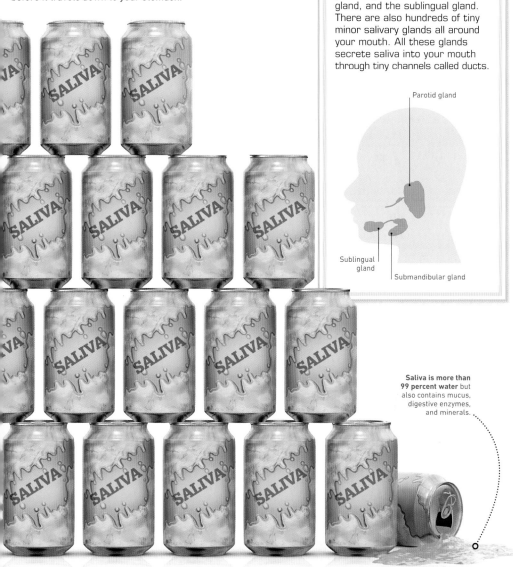

Parotid gland

Sublingual gland

Submandibular gland

Saliva is more than 99 percent water but also contains mucus, digestive enzymes, and minerals.

BRIAN KRAUSE HOLDS A WORLD RECORD FOR SPITTING A CHERRY PIT 93 FT 6.5 IN (28.51 M).

YOUR MOUTH IS HOME TO AROUND MORE THAN 6 MILLION BACTERIA.

Long **eyelashes** bat away sand, while thick **fur** protects against sunburn.

BUBBLE BLOWER

This camel uses its slimy saliva to blow bubbles that attract passing females in the desert. Life is tough for desert dwellers, but camels can survive without water for days. The humps are full of fat to provide nourishment when food runs out, and their padded feet can walk across scorching hot sand.

SOLID-LIQUID
SLIME

Not all substances behave how you would expect.
Non-Newtonian fluids are a group of substances
that can **behave like both liquids and solids,**
depending on how they are treated.

FAST FACTS

Gooey Oobleck contains long starch molecules (yellow) suspended in water (blue).

The starch and water molecules are able to flow freely past each other when no strong force is applied to the Oobleck, so it behaves like a liquid. If you gently insert your hand, it will slide between the molecules.

The water molecules are forced aside and the starch molecules stick together to form a temporary solid surface if a sudden force is applied to the Oobleck. The Oobleck will feel solid if you hit it with your fist.

"OOBLECK" COMES
FROM DR. SEUSS'S BOOK
BARTHOLOMEW AND
THE OOBLECK.

THE LONGEST TIME
SOMEONE HAS SPENT
RUNNING OVER
OOBLECK IS 1 MINUTE,
6 SECONDS.

You can dip your fingers gently into liquid Oobleck, just like water, but applying pressure turns the slime solid.

You can **scoop up** runny Oobleck and **squash it into a solid ball**.

Oobleck is a non-Newtonian fluid created by mixing cornstarch with water. Most of the time, Oobleck behaves like a typical free-flowing liquid. However, when you scoop it up and squeeze it, Oobleck feels solid. If you release the pressure, the Oobleck will return to a liquid state and trickle through your fingers.

RUNNING ON SLIME

If you make a pool of Oobleck,you could run across it! As your moving feet apply pressure to the fluid, the Oobleck will temporarily harden and feel like a solid path beneath your feet. However, you must keep moving—if you stop, the pressure will be reduced, and your feet will sink as the Oobleck behaves like a liquid again.

IN 2014, A BANK IN MALAYSIA FILLED A SMALL POOL WITH OOBLECK FOR A TV COMMERCIAL.

SCIENTISTS ARE RESEARCHING OOBLECK AS A POSSIBLE LIQUID BODY ARMOR.

SUPER-STICKY SNAIL
TRAIL

Snails may be slow movers, but there is more to these mollusks than meets the eye. Their specialized **silvery slime** allows them to **slide along surfaces and to stick to steep walls** with ease.

A snail travels along on a single, muscular "foot" that contracts and relaxes in waves to propel it forward. Glands all over the foot secrete a slimy mucus. This slime is a non-Newtonian fluid (see page 34), which means that it behaves like a solid or a liquid under different conditions. As a snail moves, contractions across its muscular foot put pressure on the slime, making it act like a liquid so it can slide along. When the snail stops moving, even up a wall, the pressure is released, and the slime solidifies to keep it stuck in place.

The snail moves along by contracting its body in wave motions. When this movement puts pressure on the slime, the slime becomes a liquid, and this helps the snail slide along.

Where no pressure is applied because the snail isn't making its muscles contract, the slime becomes more solid and sticky, which helps the snail stay stuck to the surface.

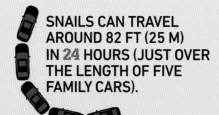

SNAILS CAN TRAVEL AROUND 82 FT (25 M) IN **24** HOURS (JUST OVER THE LENGTH OF FIVE FAMILY CARS).

THE **GIANT AFRICAN** LAND SNAIL CAN GROW TO ALMOST 15.7 IN (40 CM) IN LENGTH.

SAFE HAVEN

In warm temperatures, snails survive by withdrawing into their shells for periods known as estivation. Like hibernation, estivation is a state of dormancy, or inactivity, that protects animals from hot, dry weather by preserving their energy and water. When it estivates, a snail secretes layers of dried mucus, called epiphragms, that covers and seals the opening of its shell to prevent water loss.

Slime keeps the snail moist, protects it from such threats as bacteria and predators, and helps it move forward.

Glands all over the foot constantly secrete watery mucus.

FAST FACTS

Tomato ketchup is another example of a non-Newtonian fluid. Famously tricky to get out of a glass bottle, the thick sauce behaves like a solid most of the time. However, shaking the bottle applies force to the sauce, making it behave like a liquid so it can flow onto a plate.

SCIENTISTS HAVE CREATED A MEDICAL **GLUE** THAT MIMICS THE STICKINESS OF SNAIL SLIME.

THE **SMALLEST** SNAIL, *ANGUSTOPILA DOMINIKAE,* COULD FIT THROUGH THE EYE OF A NEEDLE.

DEADLY TONGUE
TRAP

Frogs have built-in, inescapable traps for catching dinner. Their **super-soft tongues and specialized saliva** work together to grab, grip, and pull in prey.

A frog's tongue is 10 times softer than a human tongue, so it easily wraps around prey upon impact.

Frogs can catch prey in **0.07 seconds**— five times faster than humans blink.

A CHAMELEON'S TONGUE SHOOTS OUT WITH MORE ACCELERATION THAN A SPORTS CAR.

AN INSECT PULLED INTO A FROG'S MOUTH FEELS MORE FORCE THAN AN EARTH-BOUND ASTRONAUT.

HEAVYWEIGHT TARGETS

Frogs and toads use their impressive tongues to catch large prey up to 1.4 times their own body weight. As well as insects, they may eat mice, bats, and even other frogs.

Frogs have saliva that changes between liquid and solid, depending on the pressure applied—it is a non-Newtonian fluid (see page 34). The impact of striking prey makes the saliva on their tongues runnier, allowing it to fully engulf their catch. As their tongues retract, the pressure decreases, so the saliva thickens and keeps hold.

Saliva acts like glue between the frog's tongue and the moth's body.

FAST FACTS

Frogs use a clever trick to separate prey from their sticky tongues. As they swallow, they force their eyeballs downward to put pressure on the prey, which slides the food off their tongues and down their throats.

WITH THE MOUTH CLOSED, FROG **SALIVA** ACTS LIKE A SOLID AND IS FIVE TIMES THICKER THAN HONEY.

AN AFRICAN **BULLFROG'S** TONGUE IS ABOUT THE SAME LENGTH AS THE AVERAGE HUMAN'S.

Gourmet goo

CASU MARZU CHEESE

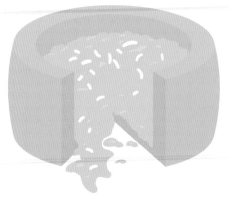

The key ingredient of this Italian cheese is the live larvae of cheese flies. To make it, cheesemakers cut a hole in the rind of wheels of sheep's milk cheese so cheese flies can lay eggs inside. When the eggs hatch, the larvae eat the cheese and break it down. Their excretions give the cheese a distinct flavor and soft texture. The average casu marzu contains thousands of the wriggling maggots!

SAGO WORMS

In Southeast Asia, the larvae of sago palm weevils, which grow to around 2 in (5 cm) long, make a tasty meal. They are popular roasted on spits to celebrate special occasions and may even be eaten alive. When served raw, their texture is gooey and creamy.

CAVIAR

Nicknamed "black gold," caviar is considered a true delicacy. These tiny eggs of sturgeon fish make a soft, squishy goo that melts in the mouth with a fresh but slightly salty flavor. The most prized caviar comes from fish in the cold waters of the Caspian Sea, between Europe and Asia, and sells for a high price in expensive restaurants around the world.

CASTOREUM

Beavers produce a fragrant substance called castoreum that they mix with urine to mark their territory. These secretions may not sound mouth-watering but were used throughout the 20th century as an additive to sweeten the flavor of some food and drinks. The use of castoreum is now rare, and synthetic flavorings are used instead.

TUNA FISH HAVE EYES THAT ARE ABOUT THE SIZE OF A TENNIS BALL.

AROUND TWO BILLION PEOPLE WORLDWIDE MUNCH ON INSECTS EVERY DAY.

HONEY

Making honey is a sticky business. After honeybees have sucked nectar from flowers, they regurgitate it into the mouths of other bees. The bees transfer it mouth-to-mouth and mix it with digestive enzymes that turn it into tasty honey. This goo is regurgitated into a honeycomb cell, where bees use their wings like a fan to remove excess water and make it even stickier.

BIRD'S NEST SOUP

Swiftlet birds make nests from their own sticky saliva, which hardens in the air. In parts of Southeast Asia, these nests are collected for chefs to dissolve in water to make goopy bird's nest soup. Although this dish is an expensive and sought-after delicacy in China, the soup can cause allergic reactions. In some areas, the collection of nests has been banned because overharvesting threatens the species. Governments have put strict regulations in place to reduce the illegal collection and sale of swiftlet nests.

ESCAMOLES

The ancient Aztecs were the first to enjoy escamoles, the edible pupae and larvae of ants. Today, the ant larvae begin their lives growing on the roots of agave plants in the Mexican desert before ending up as a tasty topping for tacos, a popular Mexican street food. Escamoles have a distinctive buttery flavor combined with a soft, gooey texture that is similar to cottage cheese.

TUNA EYES

Appearing on menus across China and Japan, tuna eyeballs can be boiled in water to give a soft, gooey consistency that allows diners to suck out the insides. The eyeballs are an excellent source of omega-3 fatty acids.

THE IRANIAN BELUGA FISH PRODUCES THE MOST EXPENSIVE **CAVIAR**—2 LB 3 OZ (1 KG) COSTS ABOUT $24,400.

ARCHAEOLOGISTS HAVE FOUND 3,000-YEAR-OLD **HONEY** THAT IS STILL EDIBLE.

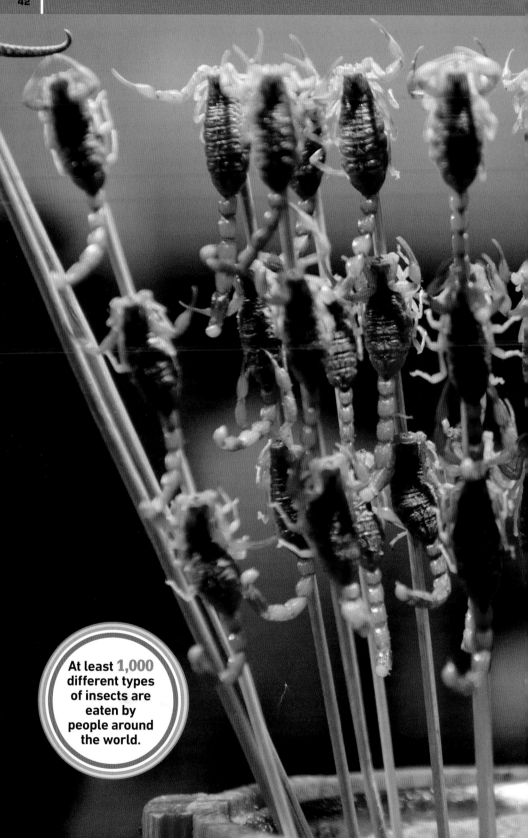

At least 1,000 different types of insects are eaten by people around the world.

EDIBLE INSECTS

Snacking on scorpions may not be everyone's idea of a tasty treat, but they are popular in parts of Asia, Africa, and Latin America. Customers can take their pick from a range of mouthwatering bugs, including ants, beetles, and mealworms. They provide essential minerals, fiber, and protein.

MUCUS
BUBBLE

Giant larvaceans are small, solitary sea creatures that inhabit all the world's oceans. They survive by filtering food from the water around them by using **delicate bubbles of mucus**.

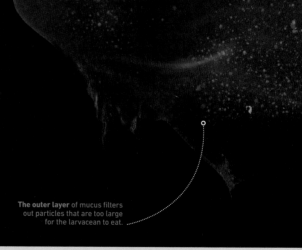

Giant larvaceans make **new mucus houses every day.**

TRANSPARENT TADPOLES

Giant larvaceans can grow to 4 in (10 cm) long, but smaller species of larvaceans may be just 0.4 in (1 cm) long. Their transparent bodies are similar in shape to tadpoles, with tails that propel them through the water. All larvaceans make delicate mucus houses to filter food from the sea water.

The outer layer of mucus filters out particles that are too large for the larvacean to eat.

ONE SPECIES OF GIANT **LARVACEAN** WASN'T SEEN AGAIN FOR OVER 100 YEARS AFTER ITS DISCOVERY IN 1900.

GIANT LARVACEANS PULL **CARBON DIOXIDE** OUT OF THE ATMOSPHERE INTO THE DEEP OCEAN.

FAST FACTS

Mucus houses gradually become heavy and blocked with the large debris they have filtered from the water. When this happens, larvaceans will leave their houses to swim off and make new ones. The discarded houses, known as "sinkers," drop to the seabed like deflated balloons and become a nutritional food source for deep-sea marine life.

The larvacean is found at the center of the bubble, and it beats its tail to move water through the mucus house.

The inner filter catches smaller, digestible food particles and guides them to the mouth of the larvacean.

Giant larvaceans use sticky mucus to filter food from the sea water. Each day they secrete blobs of mucus, which they inflate to form mucus houses. These bubbles of mucus can grow to more than 3 ft (1 m) wide. Beating their tails moves sea water through the houses, so particles of food can be filtered out for the larvaceans to eat.

 IT TAKES AROUND 45 MINUTES FOR A GIANT LARVACEAN TO BUILD ITS MUCUS HOUSE.

 **A GIANT LARVACEAN'S MUCUS HOUSE CAN FILTER UP TO 17.6 GALLONS (80 LITERS) OF WATER AN HOUR.**

LIVING
SLIME MOLD

Slime molds are **brainless but brilliant life-forms.** These **jellylike geniuses** can find food in even the trickiest situations, down to their ability to trace where they have been before.

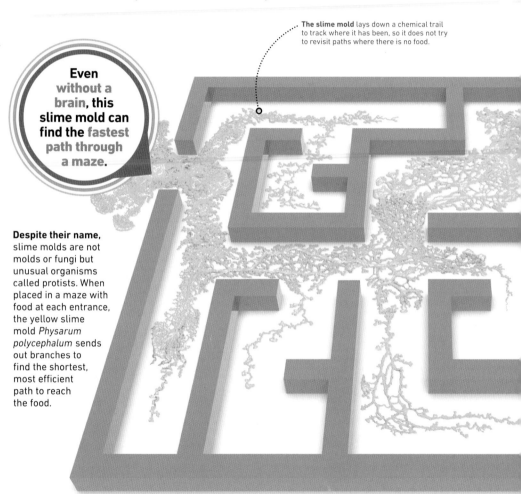

The slime mold lays down a chemical trail to track where it has been, so it does not try to revisit paths where there is no food.

Even without a brain, this slime mold can find the fastest path through a maze.

Despite their name, slime molds are not molds or fungi but unusual organisms called protists. When placed in a maze with food at each entrance, the yellow slime mold *Physarum polycephalum* sends out branches to find the shortest, most efficient path to reach the food.

SLIME MOLD SPORES CAN LAY DORMANT FOR 75 YEARS BEFORE DEVELOPING INTO NEW SLIME MOLD.

SLIME MOLDS HAVE STRANGE SHAPES AND NAMES, SUCH AS "DOG VOMIT" AND "BIRD POOP."

FOREST SLIME

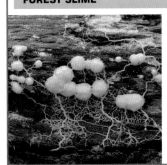

The slime mold shown at left was tested in a maze, but its usual habitat is damp woodland and forest, where it lives on rotting wood and leaf litter. Slime molds survive and grow by engulfing, and then feasting on, bacteria and fungi.

FAST FACTS

More than 1,000 species of slime mold exist around the world in a wide variety of colors, shapes, and sizes. They all look like fungi but behave more like animals as they move around searching for food.

Ceratiomyxa fruticulosa

Tubifera ferruginosa

Lycogala epidendrum

Fuligo septica

When the slime mold finds these oat flakes, it retracts itself from the paths of the maze where no food has been found and directs its growth toward the food.

In 2010, a team of researchers placed food around slime mold in positions corresponding to the locations of cities around Tokyo, Japan. They found that the slime's paths closely matched Tokyo's real rail system because it seeks the most efficient paths to food, much like transport designers seek the most efficient routes between cities.

Step 1

Step 2

Step 3 The slime mold (yellow) has found the shortest routes between food sources (white).

SLIME MOLD CAN MOVE AT SPEEDS OF UP TO 0.05 IN (1.35 MM) PER SECOND.

SOME SLIME MOLDS CAN WEIGH UP TO 44 LB (20 KG).

VOLCANIC WORLD

Io, one of Jupiter's moons, is the most volcanically active world in the solar system, with more than 400 active volcanoes. The most powerful eruptions are visible through large telescopes from Earth.

Lava from Hawaii's Mount Kilauea has reached 2,140°F (1,170°C).

OLYMPUS MONS ON MARS IS THE SOLAR SYSTEM'S LARGEST VOLCANO. IT RISES 16 MILES (25 KM).

WHEN KRAKATAU IN INDONESIA ERUPTED IN 1883, IT RELEASED THE ENERGY OF 15,000 NUCLEAR BOMBS.

The world's most active volcano is Mount Kilauea in the Hawaiian Islands. Since 1983, Mount Kilauea has been erupting almost constantly. The lava in many volcanoes is sticky and slow. However, the lava from Mount Kilauea comes from molten basalt rock, resulting in a fast-flowing fluid that covers large areas before cooling and hardening.

RIVERS OF
LIQUID ROCK

Deep beneath Earth's surface lie **chambers of scorching molten rock.** This liquid rock, called magma, can burst through the ground as volcanic eruptions and flow out in unstoppable rivers of fiery lava.

FAST FACTS

The color of heated rock can give a good indication of its temperature.

Yellow lava has a temperature of about 1,832–2,192°F (1,000–1,200°C).

Orange lava has a temperature of about 1,472–1,832°F (800–1,000°C).

Red lava has a temperature of about 1,112–1,472°F (600–800°C).

PYROCLASTIC FLOWS (AVALANCHES OF MOLTEN ROCK) CAN REACH 450 MPH (724 KMPH).

THERE ARE AROUND 1,500 ACTIVE VOLCANOES ON EARTH RIGHT NOW.

Liquefaction can make the ground so gooey it can swallow vehicles.

FAST FACTS

Liquefaction occurs when waterlogged soil is shaken so much that it loses its strength and stability.

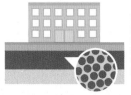

Before an earthquake hits, soil particles are loosely packed together and water fills the small spaces between them.

When shaken, the soil's structure is disturbed and soil particles flow within the surrounding water. The goopy mixture can no longer support buildings.

AN EARTHQUAKE IN NEPAL IN 2015 CAUSED MOUNT EVEREST – THE WORLD'S TALLEST MOUNTAIN – TO SHRINK.

JAPANESE MYTHOLOGY TELLS OF EARTHQUAKES BEING CAUSED BY A GIANT CATFISH.

SINKING INTO
SOIL

The full force of an earthquake can shake the ground so much that it **behaves like a thick goo.** Heavy objects may sink as the ground gives way in a process called **liquefaction**.

SHAKEN FOUNDATIONS

The Japanese city of Niigata was hit by an earthquake in 1964, leading to widespread destruction. Liquefaction meant the ground could not support buildings, leading to thousands of homes tilting dangerously and sinking into the ground.

A powerful earthquake struck the city of Christchurch, New Zealand, in 2011. As the earthquake shook the city, the saturated, or waterlogged, ground quickly became a murky sludge. This car was absorbed headfirst into the sludge, but fortunately the driver and their pet dog escaped.

THE **STRONGEST RECORDED EARTHQUAKE** (MAGNITUDE 9.5) HIT CHILE IN 1960.

LIQUEFACTION CAN OCCUR IN SOIL UP TO 66 FT (20 M) DEEP.

Sinkholes can also form underwater. They are known as marine sinkholes.

SINKING FEELING

The ground beneath your feet is usually safe and stable, but sinkholes can change that in seconds. Sinkholes are sudden gaping holes. They form when underground water dissolves limestone rock. Eventually, the rock weakens and caves in, leaving a massive, dangerous hole in the ground like this one in Japan.

Gooey medicine

YELLOW SOUP

In the 4th century, Chinese doctors cooked the dried poo of healthy people to treat people suffering from diarrhea or food poisoning. Although this yellow soup sounds unappetizing, the idea continues today — patients are sometimes treated with poo transplants from healthy donors.

BEE VENOM

In ancient Greece, the venom of bees was used to treat joint problems and arthritis as people believed it could reduce pain and swelling. These properties mean that patients in some parts of the world still use it as treatment, despite the potentially harmful effects of venom.

BODY FAT

Human fat has been used in medicine for thousands of years. A number of cultures have used fat to treat problems such as gout, broken bones, and open wounds. Animal fat has also come in handy, with goose fat used to soothe sore muscles and goat fat used to calm inflammation.

PURGING THE PLAGUE

The Black Death, an outbreak of bubonic plague, in the 1340s wiped out half the population of Europe. Symptoms of this dreadful disease included bloody, pus-filled sores on the body called buboes. Although the plague was almost always fatal, doctors tried to save lives by cutting open buboes to drain out the gooey pus.

IN **JAPAN**, PEOPLE PUT SNAILS DIRECTLY ON THEIR FACE. THE SLIME ACTS AS A FACE MASK.

IN THE 1700S, AN ENGLISH DOCTOR SUGGESTED A COUGH SYRUP MADE OF DRIED **DOG POO** AND **HONEY**.

GLADIATOR BLOOD

Epilepsy is a neurological disorder that causes seizures. Ancient Romans believed drinking the blood of the bravest men was a cure for epilepsy. In ancient Rome, mighty gladiators would fight to the death in arenas to entertain the public. The blood of the dead gladiators would be collected and consumed by epilepsy sufferers.

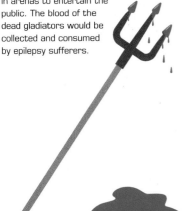

OOZING OINTMENTS

The ancient Egyptians mixed up odd ingredients to treat eye diseases. Honey blended with pig eyes and tree resin were used to heal eyes. Bats were thought to have good eyesight, so their blood was dropped into human eyes to improve vision. These treatments are not recommended today!

SNAIL SYRUP

In ancient Greece, coughs and sore throats, among other ailments, were treated using the sticky trails left behind by snails. The syrupy mucus was collected and swallowed for instant relief from sore throats and continual coughing. Even in the Middle Ages, a recommended remedy for coughs was snail slime sweetened with sugar.

AMBERGRIS (ALSO KNOWN AS WHALE VOMIT) WAS ONCE USED IN FOOD AND DRINK.

WATER SNAKE OIL HAS LONG BEEN USED IN CHINESE MEDICINE TO TREAT A NUMBER OF ILLNESSES.

PUS-FILLED
PIMPLES

Swollen spots appear on the skin when tiny openings called pores become clogged by dead skin cells. **Thick, white pus** slowly builds up inside like volcanoes ready to erupt.

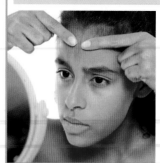

Popping pimples can be tempting, but this is the worst thing to do. Squeezing zits forces the skin to tear open, which can cause scarring, and pushes bacteria deeper into the wound, which can lead to infection.

FAST FACTS

Blackheads are another type of pimple. While whiteheads are sealed off from the air and build beneath the surface, blackheads are pimples that are not sealed off but open to the air instead. When air reaches sebum clogging up pores, the air reacts with the sebum, turning it darker. This leaves a tiny blackhead visible on the surface of the skin.

THERE ARE UP TO 900 **SEBACEOUS** GLANDS PER SQUARE CENTIMETER ON YOUR FACE, SCALP, AND CHEST.

PEOPLE WHO LIVE ON THE ISLAND OF **KITAVA** IN PAPUA NEW GUINEA NEVER GET PIMPLES.

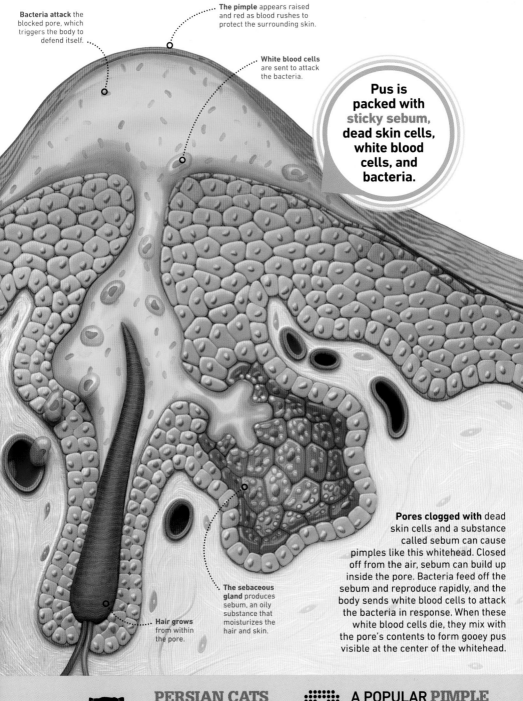

Bacteria attack the blocked pore, which triggers the body to defend itself.

The pimple appears raised and red as blood rushes to protect the surrounding skin.

White blood cells are sent to attack the bacteria.

Pus is packed with sticky sebum, dead skin cells, white blood cells, and bacteria.

Pores clogged with dead skin cells and a substance called sebum can cause pimples like this whitehead. Closed off from the air, sebum can build up inside the pore. Bacteria feed off the sebum and reproduce rapidly, and the body sends white blood cells to attack the bacteria in response. When these white blood cells die, they mix with the pore's contents to form gooey pus visible at the center of the whitehead.

The sebaceous gland produces sebum, an oily substance that moisturizes the hair and skin.

Hair grows from within the pore.

PERSIAN CATS COMMONLY GET BLACKHEADS ON THEIR FACE AND IN SKIN FOLDS.

A POPULAR **PIMPLE POPPING** VIDEO HAS HAD MORE THAN **9 MILLION** VIEWS.

STICKY
SEABIRD VOMIT

Fulmar chicks may look fluffy and feeble, but these young seabirds have a **secret weapon**. When threatened, they will **shoot smelly, sticky oil** over their attackers.

The name fulmar, meaning "foul gull", refers to the pungent orange oil the birds use as a weapon. Vulnerable chicks store this vile vomit until they need to fire it at predators, such as hungry birds. The sticky goo mats the feathers of intruding birds, and the vile smell deters any other aggressors.

PROTECTIVE PUKE

Vultures are among the few creatures that bring up their food for self-defense. If they feel threatened, they can produce highly acidic, strong-smelling vomit from their stomachs that can sting predators. Vomiting also makes the vultures lighter, enabling them to quickly fly away.

A **CONEHEAD TERMITE** DEFENDS ITSELF BY SHOOTING A STICKY **SAP** FROM ITS POINTED HEAD.

SPITTING SPIDERS CAN SPIT A DEADLY AND STICKY NET OVER A VICTIM IN A FRACTION OF A SECOND.

FAST FACTS

1.8 m (6 ft)

Fulmar chicks and adults are able to shoot their smelly stomach oil 1.8 m (6 ft). Adults use the oil as an energy source during long journeys.

Skunks also produce a smelly defensive goo. If threatened, they may shoot a foul-smelling oil from glands under their tail to ward off potential attackers.

Fulmar chicks are covered in soft, downy fluff and cannot take flight until their feathers grow, making them vulnerable to predators.

The oil **sticks like glue** to the wings of predatory birds, so they cannot fly.

CAMELS **SPIT OUT** THE CONTENTS OF THEIR STOMACH IF THEY FEEL ANNOYED OR THREATENED.

IF ATTACKED, LARGE WHITE BUTTERFLY **CATERPILLARS** SPIT SEMI-DIGESTED CABBAGE FLUID.

MUCKY
MUD BATH

Bathing does not guarantee squeaky-clean results in the animal kingdom. Some animals find themselves in a **mucky mess** instead, after **bathing in pools of sludgy mud**.

Water buffaloes use their horns to churn up the ground into mudholes.

BLOOD SWEAT

Hippopotamuses use a different goo to protect their sensitive skin, known as "blood sweat." They release a thick, red mucus through their pores that acts as a moisturizing sunscreen. It also regulates body temperature and prevents infections.

During the hot summer months, water buffaloes often submerge themselves in mud. They have very few sweat glands and run the risk of overheating, so bathing, or wallowing, in goopy, wet mud cools them down. It also provides welcome relief from the bothersome bites of mosquitoes and other bugs.

FEMALES OF A TYPE OF WASP CALLED A MUD DAUBER BUILD NESTS BY MIXING MUD WITH THEIR SALIVA.

AIR-BREATHING FISH CALLED MUDSKIPPERS BUILD BURROWS IN MUD WITH THEIR MOUTHS.

FAST FACTS

Mudholes are wildlife magnets. Even if they are only the size of small puddles, animals will work hard to turn them into massive mud baths.

Elephants roll around in mud and throw it over themselves to cool off and protect their skin from the sun.

Rhinoceroses coat themselves in mud to get rid of parasites. The bugs get stuck in the muck, and the rhinos rub against trees to scrape them off.

Tsessebes are African antelopes that perform "mud-packing." Males use their horns to sling mud at other males to establish dominance and territory.

Water buffaloes cake themselves in mud for hours in the daytime to avoid direct sunlight.

MUD **VOLCANOES**, FOUND AROUND THE WORLD, SHOOT MUD, GASES, AND STEAM UP INTO THE SKY.

HUMANS HAVE BEEN MAKING **POTTERY** FROM **MUD** FOR 30,000 YEARS.

When you inhale particles such as pollen, dust, or bacteria, the delicate lining of your nose can become irritated. Triggered by your brain, sneezing is your body's automatic response to get rid of the intruders to try to keep you healthy. Sneezes blast out watery, sticky mucus with explosive force to remove the irritants.

The droplets in sneezes travel at speeds up to 100 mph (160 kmph).

Droplets exit the mouth and nose at the same time and can reach distances of 26 ft (8 m) away.

HIGH-SPEED
SNEEZE

A single sneeze shoots **thousands of mucus droplets** through the air. These droplets can fly out **faster than cars travel on highways**. Bless you!

MARINE IGUANAS HAVE **GLANDS** THAT REMOVE SALT FROM THEIR BLOOD AND SNEEZE IT OUT OF THEIR NOSE.

WHEN HUNTING, AFRICAN **WILD DOGS** COMMUNICATE WITH EACH OTHER BY SNEEZING.

SPREADING GERMS

Sneezes can contain bacteria and viruses, including the common cold and influenza. Covering your nose and mouth when you sneeze, together with regular handwashing, helps prevent spreading these germs to other people.

Bacteria in a sneeze can stay alive in the air for as long as 45 minutes.

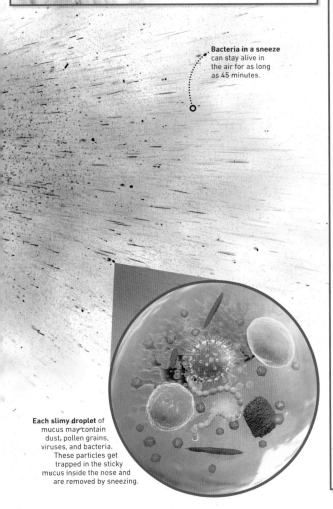

Each slimy droplet of mucus may contain dust, pollen grains, viruses, and bacteria. These particles get trapped in the sticky mucus inside the nose and are removed by sneezing.

FAST FACTS

Sneezing never happens during sleep, because the area of your brain responsible for sneezing shuts down when you are asleep.

The longest ever sneezing fit began in 1981 and lasted 976 days. British schoolgirl Donna Griffiths sneezed about one million times in the first year and continued for almost three years in total.

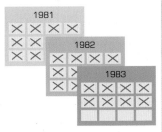

Sneezing is not the only way that humans fire mucus from their bodies at top speed.

Mucus particles released by coughing can travel at 50 mph (80 kmph).

SUDDEN EXPOSURE TO BRIGHT SUNLIGHT CAN MAKE ONE IN THREE PEOPLE SNEEZE.

THE LOUDEST RECORDED SNEEZE REACHED 176 DECIBELS—LOUDER THAN A JET ENGINE.

OOZING
RESIN

When attacked by insects or disease-causing microorganisms, some trees protect themselves by releasing **a thick goo called resin**. The substance oozes out of trees to seal their trunks against infection and invaders, like scabs forming over wounds.

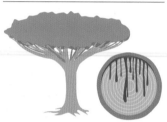
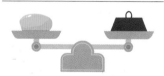
MAPLE SYRUP

The delicious sticky syrup that many people pour over their morning pancakes comes from the sap of some maple trees. Syrup harvesters hammer small taps into tree trunks and collect the sap that drips out. The collected sap is heated to concentrate it into sweet syrup.

A 99-MILLION-YEAR-OLD DINOSAUR **TAIL FEATHER** HAS BEEN FOUND PERFECTLY PRESERVED IN AMBER.

FRANKINCENSE IS A RESIN PRODUCED BY TREES FOUND IN THE MIDDLE EAST AND IS USED IN PERFUME.

Some trees, most commonly conifers, produce gluey resin. If wounded by fungi or insects, resin leaks out of the bark of these trees and hardens when exposed to the air, sealing wounds and preventing further damage. Over millions of years, resin can harden and fossilize to become amber.

If buried under the right conditions, resin may turn into beautiful orange amber.

A spider on a tree can become **trapped inside the resin** as it oozes out.

A MAPLE TREE NEEDS TO BE AT LEAST **30** YEARS OLD BEFORE IT CAN BE TAPPED FOR ITS SAP.

BALLET DANCERS PUT CRUSHED RESIN ON THEIR SHOES TO GIVE THEM A BETTER GRIP.

History of glue

200,000 YEARS AGO

Neanderthals created the first glue 200,000 years ago by burning the bark of birch trees to extract sticky tar. The adhesive was used to create tools and weapons, such as axes and spears, by gluing stone tools to wooden handles.

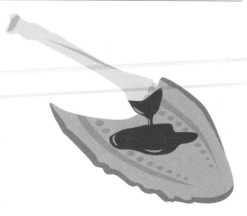

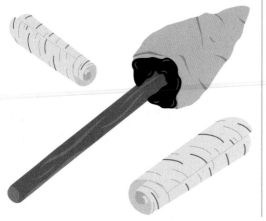

100,000 YEARS AGO

Excavations at Blombos Cave in South Africa revealed how Stone Age people made paint to decorate cave walls, their bodies, or animal skins. Brightly colored pigments from ocher in the ground were blended with gooey animal fat and marrow in the shells of sea snails. The fat may have been added to help the pigments stick to surfaces.

C. 4000 BCE

Pottery vessels discovered at ancient burial sites by archaeologists have provided evidence that ancient civilizations repaired objects with simple glues. The broken pots had been repaired with glue made from the naturally sticky sap produced by pine trees.

THE **AZTECS** OF SOUTH AMERICA USED SAP FROM DIFFERENT TYPES OF ORCHIDS TO MAKE GLUE.

ENOUGH GLUE STICKS HAVE BEEN SOLD TO LEAVE A TRAIL FROM **EARTH** TO **MARS** AND BACK.

C. 1323 BCE

Excavations of ancient Egyptian tombs revealed that glues were used in ornate furniture. Artifacts uncovered in King Tutankhamun's tomb used glue made from animal fats to stick thousands of tiny pieces of wood to furniture in decorative patterns.

1942

American researcher Dr. Harry Coover discovered a super sticky goo while working with plastics during World War II but rejected it for being too sticky. Years later, Coover and his colleague Fred Joyner experimented with the same substance, called cyanoacrylate, and saw its potential as an instant glue that could stick to almost any material. Now known as The Original Super Glue®, cyanoacrylate went on sale in 1958, changing the course of adhesive history.

THE FUTURE OF GLUE

Researchers are now looking to the natural world for adhesive inspiration. Mussels, barnacles, and oysters secrete substances that enable them to hold firmly onto wet rocks. Scientists are trying to replicate this sticky secretion to form a glue that will work underwater for ship repairs. Snail trails are also being studied— scientists are attempting to create a reversible glue that softens and stiffens in the same way as snail slime (see page 36).

1974

American scientist Arthur Fry was keen to find a way to keep his bookmark in place while singing hymns in a church choir. Remembering that a colleague, Spencer Silver, had created a light adhesive in 1968, Fry used this glue to make small paper notes that were easy to use, could stick temporarily, and could be used repeatedly. Sticky notes like these are now sold around the world.

IN THE 1700s, THE UK'S FIRST GLUE COMPANY MADE GLUE OUT OF FISH SKIN AND BONES.

18

AN 18.7-TON TRUCK WAS HELD OFF THE GROUND FOR ONE HOUR WITH SUPER-STRONG GLUE.

GOOEY GUM

The world's gooiest Gum Wall takes center-stage at Pike Place Market in Seattle, WA. This is the combined efforts of thousands of people stopping and sticking their colorful, chewed gum on the same brick wall since 1993. The mucus masterpiece measures 50 ft (15 m) in length and made it into the top five germiest tourist attractions in 2009!

The wall was cleaned once in 2015, when **2,350 lb (1,065 kg)** of gum was removed.

Sundews can take **months** to **fully digest their prey.**

FLYPAPER
PLANT

Sundews are pretty plants with big appetites and **can kill insects in minutes**. Attracted by the colors and fragrances of the plants, insects get **stuck in their gluey goo** before being slowly digested.

Each tiny tentacle on this leaf is coated in gooey mucilage. This mucilage contains enzymes that will digest any trapped prey.

Sundews are a carnivorous plant species found around the world. They secrete a sweet, gluey substance called mucilage at the tips of their red tentacles to entice and trap passing prey. When insects, like this fly, get stuck in the mucilage on the tentacles, the leaves coil tightly around them. Powerful enzymes in the mucilage slowly digest the prey, and the plants then absorb the nutritious remains.

SCIENTISTS HAVE COPIED SUNDEW'S STICKY GOO AND CREATED A GEL THAT HELPS HEAL WOUNDS.

HARDWICKE'S WOOLLY BATS LIVE IN PITCHER PLANT JUGS. THEIR DROPPINGS HELP FEED THE PLANT.

FAST FACTS

It takes 15 minutes for sundews to kill trapped insects, although the entire digestion process takes much longer.

Sundews are well adapted to attract and capture unsuspecting insects that come too close to their deadly, gooey traps.

A fly becomes stuck in the sundew's gluey mucilage and begins to struggle.

The struggling fly gets stuck to even more tentacles. The leaf begins to wrap around the fly, killing it.

The fly is broken down by the digestive juices in the mucilage and is absorbed by the plant.

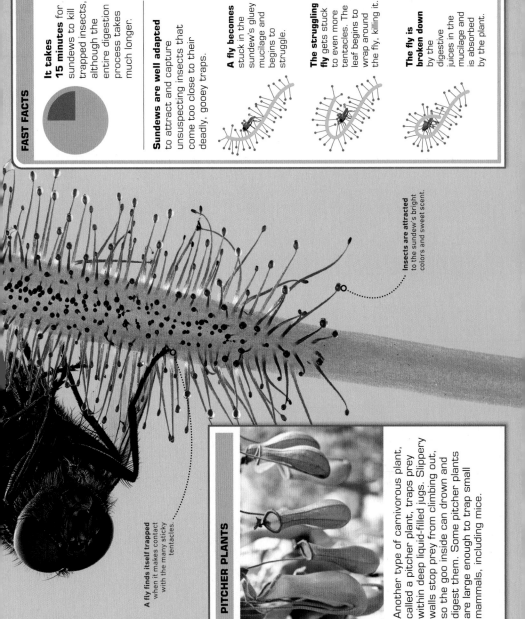

Insects are attracted to the sundew's bright colors and sweet scent.

A fly finds itself trapped when it makes contact with the many sticky tentacles.

PITCHER PLANTS

Another type of carnivorous plant, called a pitcher plant, traps prey within deep liquid-filled jugs. Slippery walls stop prey from climbing out, so the goo inside can drown and digest them. Some pitcher plants are large enough to trap small mammals, including mice.

ATTENBOROUGH'S PITCHER PLANT CAN REACH 4.9 FT (1.5 M) TALL.

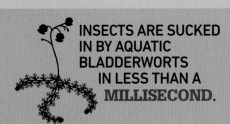

INSECTS ARE SUCKED IN BY AQUATIC BLADDERWORTS IN LESS THAN A **MILLISECOND.**

SPINNERETS AND SPIGOTS

Spiders have silk-spinning organs on their abdomens called spinnerets. Silk threads are pulled through tiny nozzlelike openings on their spinnerets called spigots. The size of these openings can be altered to change the strength, thickness, and texture of the silk as it is pulled through, depending on its purpose.

STICKY
SPIDER SILK

The silk secreted by spiders begins as a **thick goo.** As it is drawn out of their bodies, it alters to become sticky, waterproof, elastic, and **tougher than any other natural or synthetic fiber on Earth**.

FAST FACTS

Spiders produce and store silk in silk glands. The gel-like liquid is drawn from the glands through narrow channels, where it is converted to a solid. The silk can then be drawn out as a strong thread through organs called spinnerets. Spiders can have a number of silk glands, and each gland will produce silk with different properties and functions.

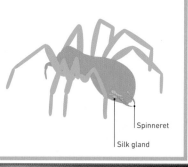

Spinneret

Silk gland

SPIDER SILK IS LIGHTER THAN COTTON AND 200 TIMES THINNER THAN HUMAN HAIR.

DARWIN'S BARK SPIDER SPINS THE WORLD'S LARGEST WEB, SPANNING UP TO **82 FT** (25 M).

As spiders draw gooey silk out of their bodies, it turns into a solid silk strand in under a second. *Argiope aurantia* spiders from the Americas can produce several different types of silk for different purposes, such as weaving sticky webs, creating sacs to protect their eggs, and encasing prey like this cricket.

Spiders can produce up to seven different types of silk to suit a range of uses.

This silk is stretchy and strong, so it is used to bind prey for the spider to eat later.

Silk webs lose their stickiness within a day, so spiders sometimes eat their webs to make use of some of the energy and protein that they contain.

SOME SPIDERS SPIN **SILK SAILS** THAT CAN CARRY THEM ACROSS OCEANS.

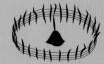

SPIDERS FROM SOUTH AMERICA BUILD **SILKHENGE** STRUCTURES THAT PROTECT THEIR EGGS.

WONDER WEB

It takes only 30 minutes for North America's orb weaver spider to create this enormous wheel-shaped web from scratch. First, the spider assesses the area for suitable anchor points before getting to work, spinning strong, sticky silk for its incredible feat of engineering. The orb weaver spider can build a web of this size every day, setting a perfect trap for passing victims.

The orb weaver web can trap up to 250 insects a day.

SEA
SLIME

The world's oceans are home to a host of **slime-squirting sea creatures** that have developed ingenious ways of using **goo to get by.**

Sea hares are soft-bodied mollusks found in shallow coastal waters that release toxic clouds of ink to scare and distract predators. The goo includes a sticky mixture of chemicals called opaline. When this opaline sticks to the antennae of attackers, it masks their senses and stops them in their tracks.

Sea cucumbers can quickly regenerate their sticky organs.

VAMPIRE SQUID EAT DEAD SEA CREATURES, POO, AND SNOT, ALL GLUED TOGETHER WITH THEIR OWN MUCUS.

CLOWN FISH COVER THEMSELVES IN **MUCUS** AS PROTECTION FROM THE TENTACLES OF THE STINGING ANEMONE.

Shallow Caribbean waters shine at night as little crustaceans called ostracods produce glowing blue mucus. The production and emission of light by living organisms is called bioluminescence. Male ostracods secrete their glowing mucus in courtship displays to attract females. The bioluminescence can also be used to scare away predators.

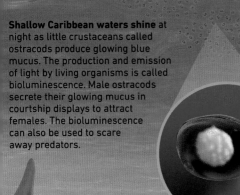

Jellyfish are unusual animals that have roamed Earth's oceans for more than 500 million years and have survived multiple mass extinctions. The simple, squishy creatures are 95 percent water and just 5 percent solid matter. Some species can grow to giant sizes—the lion's mane jellyfish can stretch as long as 120 ft (37 m).

Hagfish are eel-like marine fish that produce messy mucus to defend themselves from predators. They will release a teaspoon of mucus, which can expand to become 10,000 times larger within a fraction of a second. The stringy goo blocks the gills and throats of predators, giving the hagfish time to escape.

Parrot fish prepare for sleep by secreting large bags of slimy mucus from glands in their gill cavities to surround their bodies. Scientists are not sure why the fish create these cocoons, but they are thought to protect the fish from tiny parasites and larger predators.

Some sea cucumbers have an extraordinary method of self-defense. When under attack, they discharge some of their internal organs through the anus. Predators become tangled in these thread-like organs, which stick to them like glue.

WHEN THREATENED, **MANDARINFISH** EXCRETE A **TOXIC**, STINKY SLIME FROM SPINES ON THE SKIN.

GREEN **MORAY EELS** ARE BLUE BUT ARE COATED IN YELLOW **SLIME** THAT MAKES THEM LOOK GREEN.

BLOOMING
GOO

Under the right conditions, a type of microscopic bacteria called cyanobacteria can cover huge expanses of water with **gunky green goo** that looks like **giant puddles of pea soup**.

BUMPER BLOOM

Cyanobacteria blooms in Lake Erie can be seen from space. One bloom in 2017 reached 700 sq miles (1,800 sq km), an area larger than 250,000 football fields.

Slimy cyanobacteria can produce toxins harmful to humans and animals.

BACTERIA BLOOMS IN THE OCEAN (CALLED "MILKY SEAS") CAN SPAN 5,792 SQ MILES (15,000 SQ KM).

FOODS SUCH AS YOGURT, CHEESE, MISO, AND KIMCHI ARE ALL MADE WITH BACTERIA.

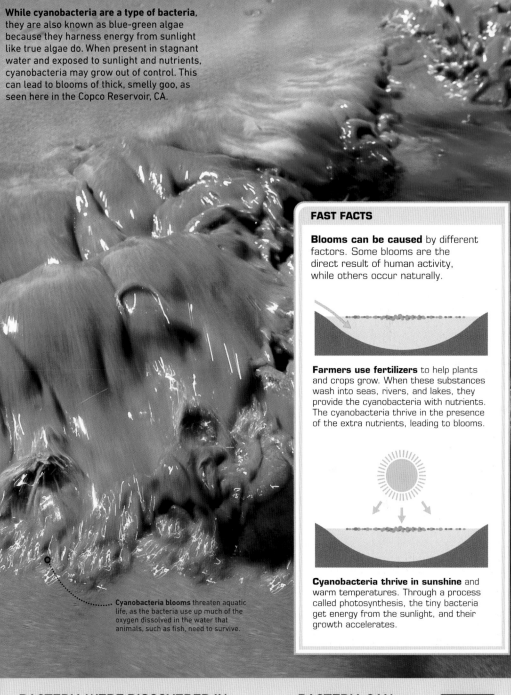

While cyanobacteria are a type of bacteria, they are also known as blue-green algae because they harness energy from sunlight like true algae do. When present in stagnant water and exposed to sunlight and nutrients, cyanobacteria may grow out of control. This can lead to blooms of thick, smelly goo, as seen here in the Copco Reservoir, CA.

Cyanobacteria blooms threaten aquatic life, as the bacteria use up much of the oxygen dissolved in the water that animals, such as fish, need to survive.

FAST FACTS

Blooms can be caused by different factors. Some blooms are the direct result of human activity, while others occur naturally.

Farmers use fertilizers to help plants and crops grow. When these substances wash into seas, rivers, and lakes, they provide the cyanobacteria with nutrients. The cyanobacteria thrive in the presence of the extra nutrients, leading to blooms.

Cyanobacteria thrive in sunshine and warm temperatures. Through a process called photosynthesis, the tiny bacteria get energy from the sunlight, and their growth accelerates.

BACTERIA WERE DISCOVERED IN 1674 BY ANTONIE VAN LEEUWENHOEK USING HIS MICROSCOPE.

BACTERIA CAN SURVIVE EXTREME TEMPERATURES AND RADIOACTIVE WASTE.

All about poo

A trip to the toilet keeps
your body firing on all cylinders.
But precious poo can be put
to good use in all kinds of ways,
so hold your nose and waste
not, want not!

Dung beetles are the strongest—and
smelliest—insects on Earth! They pounce
on poop to suck up the nutrients and moisture.
They also dig tunnels under poo piles and
fight rivals for prized poo.

FAST FACTS

24–48 hours

It takes 24–48 hours for your digestive system to turn a meal into a poo.

Large intestine

Rectum

Your intestines have muscles that squeeze food and poo to push them along. When they do this, you hear your belly rumbling.

Airway shuts

Pushing out poo uses lots of muscles, including those in your chest! Your chest muscles squeeze your lungs, but the airway that lets air escape shuts. This makes your lungs push down on your intestine.

HOW IS
POO MADE?

Poo is made by your body's **digestive system**—a set of organs that work together to break down food into molecules your body can absorb.

1. Your tongue and teeth mash food into a pulp, and chemicals in your saliva (spit) start to break it down.

2. When you swallow, mouthfuls of food are squeezed down a long tube (the esophagus) to your stomach.

IF EMPTY, YOUR STOMACH IS THE SIZE OF A TENNIS BALL. IT CAN EXPAND TO FOOTBALL SIZE WHEN FULL.

PLATYPUSES HAVE NO STOMACH. THEIR THROAT RUNS STRAIGHT TO THEIR INTESTINE.

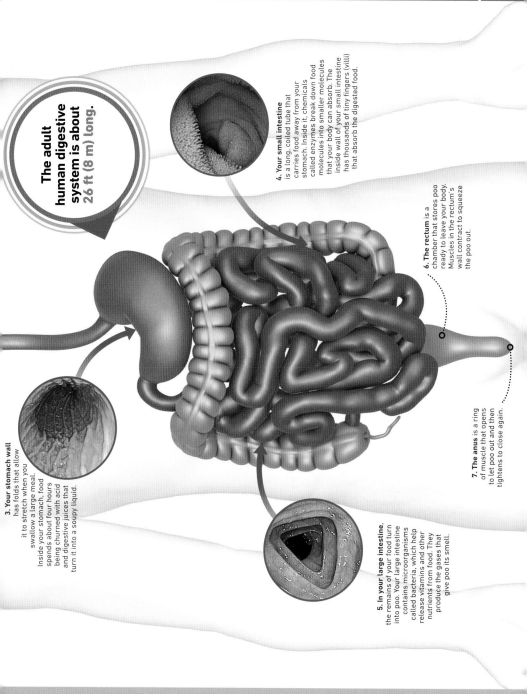

The adult human digestive system is about 26 ft (8 m) long.

4. Your small intestine is a long, coiled tube that carries food away from your stomach. Inside it, chemicals called enzymes break down food molecules into smaller molecules that your body can absorb. The inside wall of your small intestine has thousands of tiny fingers (villi) that absorb the digested food.

6. The rectum is a chamber that stores poo ready to leave your body. Muscles in the rectum's wall contract to squeeze the poo out.

7. The anus is a ring of muscle that opens to let poo out and then tightens to close again.

3. Your stomach wall has folds that allow it to stretch when you swallow a large meal. Inside your stomach, food spends about four hours being churned with acid and digestive juices that turn it into a soupy liquid.

5. In your large intestine, the remains of your food turn into poo. Your large intestine contains microorganisms called bacteria, which help release vitamins and other nutrients from food. They produce the gases that give poo its smell.

THE **TOTAL AREA** OF A HUMAN'S INTESTINES IS ABOUT HALF THE SIZE OF A BADMINTON COURT.

IT TAKES ABOUT **7 SECONDS** FOR FOOD TO TRAVEL DOWN THE ESOPHAGUS TO THE STOMACH.

WHAT'S
POO MADE OF?

Poo isn't just undigested food. About **half its weight** consists of **microscopic organisms** called bacteria. They come from your microbiome—an ecosystem of organisms living in and on your body.

Live bacteria make up about a quarter of poo. Poo is a living substance, with more than 1,000 species of bacteria. It also contains smaller numbers of viruses, fungi, and microorganisms called protists and archaea.

DIETARY FIBER

Dietary fiber helps keep you healthy by feeding friendly bacteria in your large intestine and by making poo bulkier and therefore easier to push along. Foods rich in fiber include beans, wholewheat, and vegetables such as corn.

An average human poo contains about 250 microscopic particles of plastic.

GREEN VEGETABLES CAN TURN POO GREEN. BEETS CAN TURN IT A (HARMLESS) BLOOD-RED COLOR.

PRECIOUS METALS SUCH AS GOLD ARE FOUND IN POO. A FORTUNE IN VALUE IS FLUSHED DOWN THE TOILET.

Inorganic compounds such as calcium and iron salts make up about 7% of poo. They come from your food, your digestive juices, and the layer of slimy mucus that coats the insides of your intestines.

Fiber from plant foods makes up about 6% of poo. Our bodies can't digest fiber, but some of the bacteria in the human microbiome can.

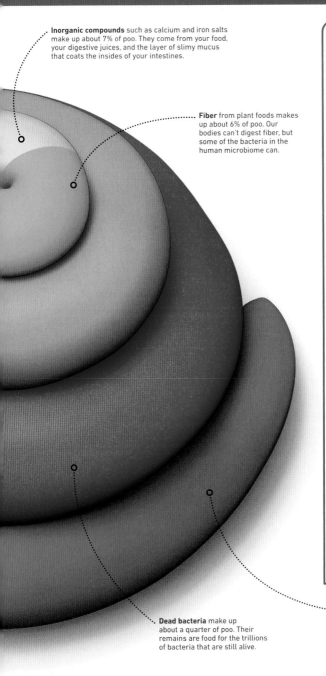

FAST FACTS

Cow dung contains plenty of microbes but little plant fiber. That's because cows have special stomachs housing bacteria and archaea that digest the fiber in grass.

Rabbit droppings have lots of bacteria and lots of plant fiber. Unlike cows, rabbits can't digest fiber in their stomachs and instead rely on microbes living in their large intestine.

Bird droppings are packed with bacteria from their large intestine. Birds mix their poo and pee together, which is why their droppings have black (poo) and white (pee) patches.

Dead bacteria make up about a quarter of poo. Their remains are food for the trillions of bacteria that are still alive.

Water makes up just over one-third of the weight of poo. Your intestines also secrete a slippery, watery fluid called mucus onto the surface of poo to help it slide along.

IN ONE YEAR, A PERSON CAN PRODUCE **161 LB** (73 KG) OF POO—ABOUT THE WEIGHT OF A BIG DOG.

DARK COLORED VEGETABLES SUCH AS ARTICHOKES AND BROCCOLI ARE SUPER RICH IN FIBER.

HOW MANY BACTERIA
ARE THERE
IN ONE POO?

A poo of average size **contains a mind-boggling** 10,000,000,000,000 (ten trillion) bacteria as well as billions of other microorganisms.

POO VIRUSES

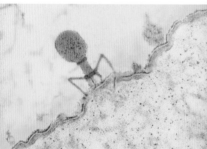

Even smaller than the bacteria in poo are viruses—the smallest life-forms on Earth. One level teaspoon of poo contains up to 5 billion viruses. Most are bacteriophages—viruses that attack bacteria. Built like tiny spacecraft, complete with landing legs, they land on bacteria and inject their own genes to take over the cell.

IF YOU LINED UP ALL OF EARTH'S BACTERIA, THEY WOULD STRETCH **10 BILLION** LIGHT-YEARS INTO SPACE.

E. COLI, A TYPE OF BACTERIA, CAN TRAVEL **25 TIMES** ITS OWN LENGTH IN ONE SECOND.

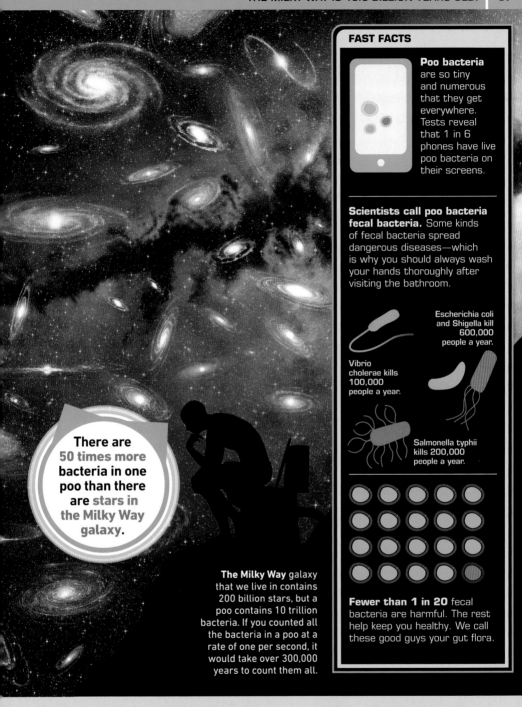

> There are **50 times more** bacteria in one poo than there are **stars in the Milky Way** galaxy.

The Milky Way galaxy that we live in contains 200 billion stars, but a poo contains 10 trillion bacteria. If you counted all the bacteria in a poo at a rate of one per second, it would take over 300,000 years to count them all.

FAST FACTS

Poo bacteria are so tiny and numerous that they get everywhere. Tests reveal that 1 in 6 phones have live poo bacteria on their screens.

Scientists call poo bacteria fecal bacteria. Some kinds of fecal bacteria spread dangerous diseases—which is why you should always wash your hands thoroughly after visiting the bathroom.

Escherichia coli and Shigella kill 600,000 people a year.

Vibrio cholerae kills 100,000 people a year.

Salmonella typhii kills 200,000 people a year.

Fewer than 1 in 20 fecal bacteria are harmful. The rest help keep you healthy. We call these good guys your gut flora.

SCIENTISTS HAVE MADE BACTERIA ACT LIKE **COMPUTERS**, PROGRAMMING THEM TO PERFORM TASKS.

THE WORD **VIRUS** COMES FROM THE LATIN WORD MEANING **"POISON"** OR **"SLIMY LIQUID."**

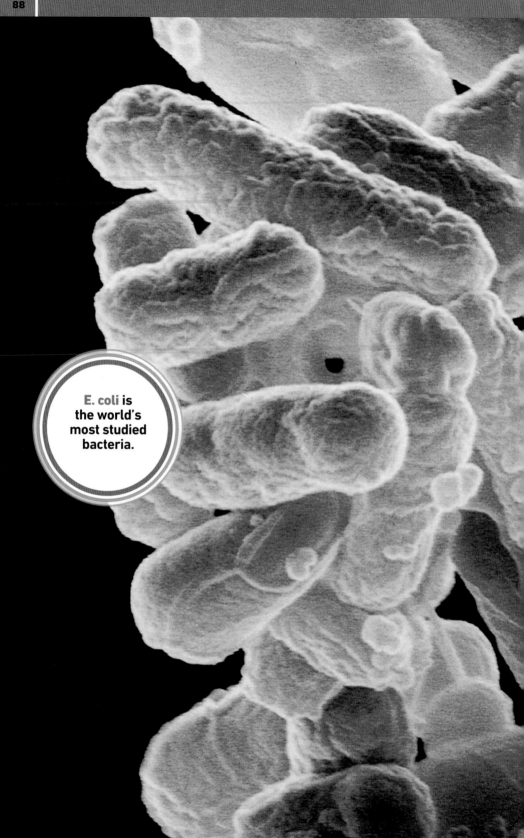

E. coli is the world's most studied bacteria.

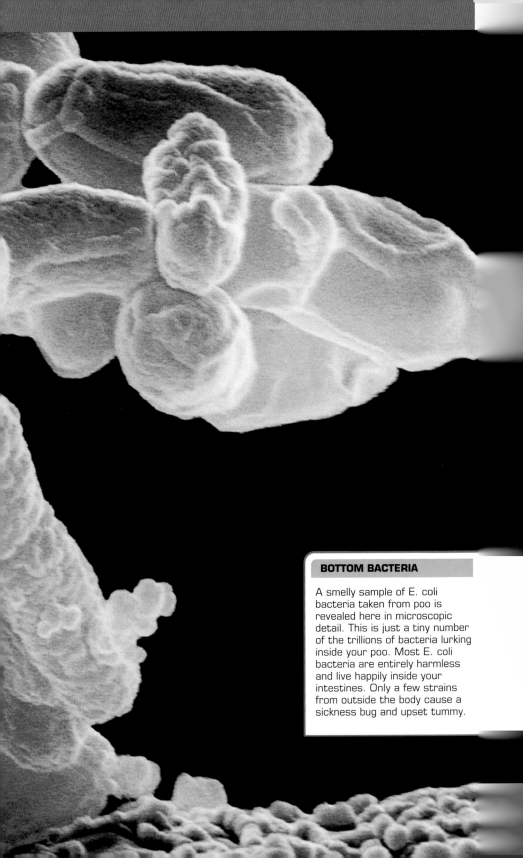

BOTTOM BACTERIA

A smelly sample of E. coli bacteria taken from poo is revealed here in microscopic detail. This is just a tiny number of the trillions of bacteria lurking inside your poo. Most E. coli bacteria are entirely harmless and live happily inside your intestines. Only a few strains from outside the body cause a sickness bug and upset tummy.

LIFE ON
THE TOILET

Most people poo **once a day**, which adds up to about 29,000 number twos in a lifetime. If it takes you **five minutes** each time, you'll spend **100 days of your life** pooing.

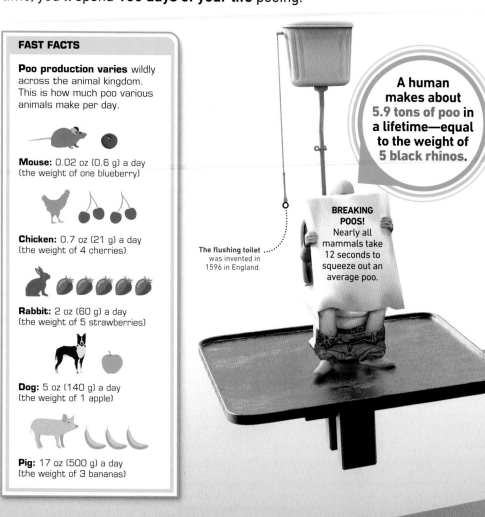

FAST FACTS

Poo production varies wildly across the animal kingdom. This is how much poo various animals make per day.

Mouse: 0.02 oz (0.6 g) a day (the weight of one blueberry)

Chicken: 0.7 oz (21 g) a day (the weight of 4 cherries)

Rabbit: 2 oz (60 g) a day (the weight of 5 strawberries)

Dog: 5 oz (140 g) a day (the weight of 1 apple)

Pig: 17 oz (500 g) a day (the weight of 3 bananas)

A human makes about 5.9 tons of poo in a lifetime—equal to the weight of 5 black rhinos.

The flushing toilet was invented in 1596 in England.

BREAKING POOS! Nearly all mammals take 12 seconds to squeeze out an average poo.

THE FIRST PUBLIC RESTROOM TO HAVE FLUSHING TOILETS OPENED IN THE 1850s IN LONDON, ENGLAND.

A TOILET-THEMED RESTAURANT IN TAIWAN SERVES SOUP IN TOILET-SHAPED BOWLS.

Poo size varies a lot from person to person, but the average adult human produces about 7 oz (200 g) a day. Over an average 79-year lifespan, that amounts to the weight of five black rhinos. By contrast, an African elephant can drop up to 485 lb (220 kg) a day—up to 1,000 times more than a human.

All the rhinos in the same area poo in a single communal heap called a dung midden.

Rhinos may be built like tanks, but they can reach 34 mph (55 kmph) in a sprint, which is 50% faster than the world's top Olympic sprinter.

DOGGIE DIRECTION

Scientists have found that dogs prefer to face north when pooing. This may be because dogs use poo pit stops to recalibrate their internal compass, which they use to find their way around.

CHINA'S **PORCELAIN PALACE** IS A FOUR-STORY PUBLIC BATHROOM WITH MORE THAN 1,000 TOILETS.

ACCORDING TO POLLS, 90% OF PEOPLE TAKE THEIR **PHONE** TO THE TOILET WITH THEM.

HOW MUCH POO
HAS BEEN POOED?

Over the course of history, the **human race has pooed** a grand total of about 196.8 billion tons (200 billion metric tons) of poo.

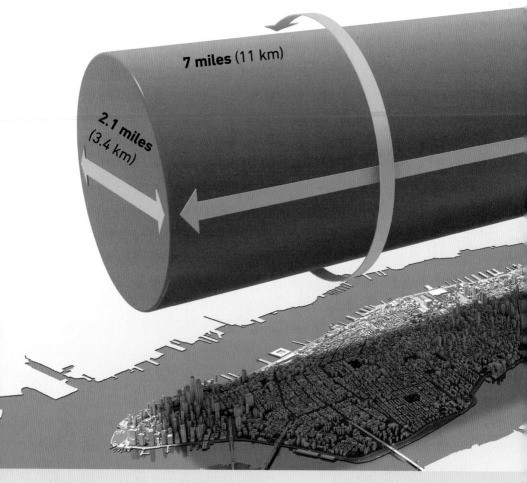

7 miles (11 km)

2.1 miles (3.4 km)

IN ONE DAY, THE **WORLD'S POO** WOULD FILL ABOUT 417 OLYMPIC-SIZED SWIMMING POOLS.

A **BLUE WHALE** CAN **EXCRETE** UP TO 44 GALLONS (200 LITERS) AT ONCE.

FAST FACTS

The total weight of all human poo in history is about the same as the weight of Mount Everest from base camp to summit.

Mount Everest   Mount Poo

Annual poo volume

10,000 BCE   Today

The quantity of poo the world makes has risen dramatically along with population growth. Every year, we poo more in a year than ever before.

14 miles (22 km)

All the poo in history would make a single log as long and wide as **Manhattan Island** in New York.

POO LENGTH

Big cities like New York City have to deal with an ever-increasing volume of poo as their populations grow. All over the world, cities are expanding and upgrading their sewers to manage the never-ending flow of waste.

If all the poo that humans have ever produced were joined into a single unbroken poo of average width, it would be 81 billion miles (130 billion km) long, which is long enough to stretch to the sun and back more than 400 times.

THE WORLD'S LONGEST HUMAN POO BELONGED TO A 1,200-YEAR-OLD VIKING. IT WAS **8 IN** (20 CM) LONG.

ALL OF THE DOGS IN AUSTRALIA PRODUCE THE WEIGHT OF **NINE JUMBO JETS** IN POO EVERY DAY.

WHAT IS
PEE?

Pee is a mix of water your body doesn't need and **thousands of waste chemicals** produced by your body's cells. It's made by two organs, called kidneys, that continually filter and clean your blood.

Scientists have identified more than 3,000 waste chemicals in human pee.

FAST FACTS

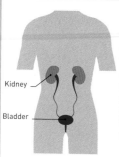

Kidney

Bladder

Every minute, a quarter of the blood in your body passes through your kidneys. They filter out waste chemicals and water that your body doesn't need. The resulting liquid drains into a storage organ called the bladder.

Size of an empty bladder

Half full

Size of a full bladder

Your bladder expands like a balloon as it fills up with pee. An empty bladder is about the size of a plum, but a full bladder is as big as a grapefruit. The bladder's wall is made of muscle that squeezes to make the pee shoot out.

 YOUR **BLADDER** CAN HOLD 0.8 PT (0.5 LITER) OF URINE FOR ABOUT 5 HOURS BEFORE YOU NEED TO PEE.

 IN ANCIENT ROME, **URINE** WAS USED TO **BLEACH** WOOL AND LINEN AND TAN LEATHER.

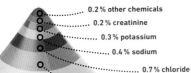

0.2 % other chemicals

0.2 % creatinine

0.3 % potassium

0.4 % sodium

0.7 % chloride
Sodium and chloride
make up common salt.

3.2 % urea
This is the main waste chemical
in pee and comes from the
breakdown of proteins.

URINE X-RAY

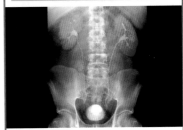

Doctors can check that your
kidneys are working properly by
giving you a special kind of X-ray
that makes pee visible. First
the doctor injects your blood
with a chemical called iodine,
which shows up on X-rays. A
few minutes later, your kidneys
will have removed the iodine
from your blood, making
your kidneys and bladder
visible on an X-ray.

90–98 % water

Human pee is an
incredibly complicated
liquid, with a chemical
makeup that changes by
the hour. However, the
vast majority of it is water.
If you drink too much water,
your blood becomes dilute, and
your kidneys respond by taking
more water out of it. So, as well as
getting rid of waste, your kidneys
keep your body's water level in
perfect balance all the time.

CAT PEE
CONTAINS A LOT
OF PHOSPHORUS
AND CAN GLOW
UNDER UV LIGHT.

CHINESE
SOFTSHELL
TURTLES PEE
MOSTLY THOUGH
THEIR MOUTHS.

HOW MUCH PEE
HAS BEEN PEED?

The human race has peed a mind-boggling 336 cubic miles (**1,400 cubic kilometers**) of pee throughout the whole of human history.

Enough pee has been peed to keep North America's **Niagara Falls** flowing for **18.5 years.**

KANGAROO RAT

Desert animals like the kangaroo rat pee very little because they can't afford to waste any water. The kangaroo rat never drinks water. Instead, its body creates water chemically by breaking down food molecules in its cells, which produces water and carbon dioxide as waste products.

Niagara Falls on the US–Canada border is the most powerful waterfall in North America. Every second, 630,000 gallons (2.4 million liters) of water gush over the towering cliff.

THE LONGEST A PERSON HAS PEED **CONTINUOUSLY** IS 508 SECONDS (OR 8.5 MINUTES).

THERE'S AROUND 20 GALLONS (90 LITERS) OF PEE IN THE AVERAGE **SWIMMING POOL.**

FAST FACTS

On average, the human body produces 3 pints (1.4 liters) of pee every day. That's enough to fill two bathtubs in a year.

The color of pee depends on how much water you drink. The less water, the darker your pee. The color comes from the chemical urochrome, produced when old blood cells are recycled.

A **FIN WHALE** CAN PEE UP TO 257 GALLONS (974 LITERS) IN ONE DAY.

BIRDS DON'T PEE. THE UREA IS TURNED INTO **URIC ACID** AND EMITTED FROM THE ANUS.

HOW MUCH GAS DO YOU PASS
IN A LIFETIME?

The bacteria in your intestines **produce a lot of gas,** and it has to go somewhere. Every day, an average 1.5 pints (700 ml) of **gas erupts** from the human anus. Over a lifetime, you pass about 5,000 gallons (20,000 liters) of gas.

FAST FACTS

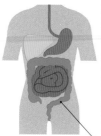

Farts are made by bacteria in your large intestine. They use a process called fermentation to break down fiber in food, producing gases as waste products.

Large intestine

Foods rich in fiber

Foods that make you fart more are good for you because they include lots of fiber. Although these foods increase the volume of farts, they don't make them smelly. The smell comes from foods rich in sulfur, such as meat and dairy foods.

You pass enough gas in your life to fill 2,000 party balloons.

GAS TRAVELS THROUGH THE AIR AT ABOUT 7 MPH (11 KMPH).

MANATEES USE THEIR FARTS TO HELP THEM SINK OR FLOAT IN THE SEA.

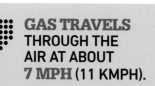

Most people fart about 8–12 times a day, but some people toot hundreds of times. A typical fart consists mostly of odorless gases, including hydrogen, carbon dioxide, and nitrogen. Smells come from tiny quantities of sulfur gases, which make up less than 1 percent of a fart.

ANIMALS THAT DON'T FART

Not every kind of animal farts. Sloths make gas in their intestine, but the gas is absorbed by their blood and breathed out. Birds have never been seen farting. This might be because they digest food so quickly that gases cannot build up.

 AROUND **20** PEOPLE COMPETE IN THE **WORLD FARTING** CHAMPIONSHIPS IN FINLAND EVERY YEAR.

 A CLOTHES COMPANY HAS CREATED **UNDERWEAR** THAT FILTERS THE SMELL OF YOUR FARTS.

Toilet data

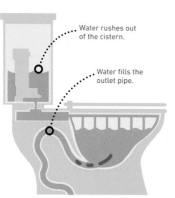

A tank called a cistern stores water for flushing.

Bowl

Double bend

Water trapped by bendy outlet

Poo

Flushing toilets that blocked smells were invented more than 200 years ago. Before then, toilets were too smelly to keep in the home. A simple but ingenious invention solved the problem: a **double bend** in the outlet pipe traps water, blocking smells from the sewer. In many flushing toilets, the outlet pipe also works as a siphon—a pipe that sucks water when it's full. Siphonic toilets suck waste out of the bowl after flushing and then make a noisy gurgle before the bowl refills with water again.

1. Before flushing
the bowl is full of water, forming an odor seal.

Water rushes out of the cistern.

Water fills the outlet pipe.

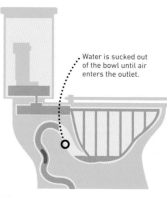

Water is sucked out of the bowl until air enters the outlet.

2. When you flush, water surges into the bowl, washing out the waste. The outlet pipe fills, triggering the siphon effect.

3. The siphon effect sucks water out of the bowl until air enters the outlet pipe. The air stops the siphon effect and causes a gurgling sound. The bowl then refills with water.

A TEAM OF STUDENTS BUILT A **MOTORIZED** TOILET THAT REACHED A RECORD 70.5 MPH (113.5 KMPH).

GERMS FROM A FLUSHING TOILET CAN BE THROWN 6 FT (183 CM) INTO THE AIR.

BIDET TOILET

Warm water jet

Control panel

The latest **electronic toilets** make toilet paper unnecessary. They shoot a precisely aimed jet of warm water at the user, followed by a blast of air from a blow dryer. Called bidet toilets, some also feature electrically warmed seats and loudspeakers that play music or flushing sounds to mask embarrassing body noises.

PIT LATRINE

Around **1.8 billion of the world's people** use a large hole in the ground instead of a flushing toilet connected to a sewer. This type of toilet is called a pit latrine. If the pit is large and deep enough, it lasts for years before a new one has to be dug.

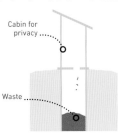

Cabin for privacy

Waste

COMPOST TOILET

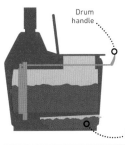

A composting toilet turns poo into compost. Waste is stored in a rotating drum that must be turned several times a week. When it's more than half full, contents are released into a finishing drawer, where they spend a month turning into compost.

Drum handle

Finishing drawer

INCINERATOR

In remote places without sewers, poo can't be flushed away. Incinerating toilets solve the problem by **burning poo** in a built-in oven and turning it into ash. Because the bowl isn't flushed with water, it's lined with fresh paper each time you use it.

Chimney

Paper-lined bowl

Inlet pushes poo into oven

Oven

SUCTION TOILET

To save on water, toilets in planes use **powerful suction** to empty toilets. The suction is created by pumps or by vents that connect the waste storage tank to the exterior, where the air pressure is much lower than inside the plane.

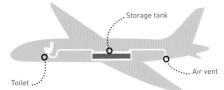

Storage tank

Air vent

Toilet

FREEZER TOILET

A **freezer toilet** freezes waste until it can be disposed of. Poo drops into a bucket lined with a biodegradable bag and is chilled to subzero temperatures by refrigerant gases, just like food in a freezer.

Poo

Freezer

FROZEN POO, KNOWN AS BLUE ICE, OCCASIONALLY LEAKS AND FALLS FROM AIRPLANES.

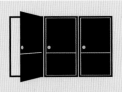

THE FIRST CUBICLE IN A PUBLIC TOILET IS THE LEAST USED AND THEREFORE THE CLEANEST.

HOW MUCH TOILET PAPER
DOES THE
WORLD USE?

The Vikings used snow, the Romans used a sponge on a stick, and sailors used a wet rope. Today, **most people** in the Western world use **toilet paper** for personal hygiene.

> Every hour, the world uses enough toilet paper to wrap around the planet 14 times.

Toilet paper was invented in China more than 1,400 years ago, but it took a long time to catch on. Mass-produced brands, marketed as "splinter-free," became widespread in Europe and North America only a century ago. Today, paper is most popular in colder parts of the world, while people in hot countries often use water for washing and paper just for drying, if at all.

AN AUSTRALIAN COMPANY MADE A GOLD TOILET PAPER THEY HOPED TO SELL FOR THOUSANDS.

DAVID RUSH HOLDS THE WORLD RECORD FOR BALANCING 101 TOILET ROLLS ON HIS HEAD.

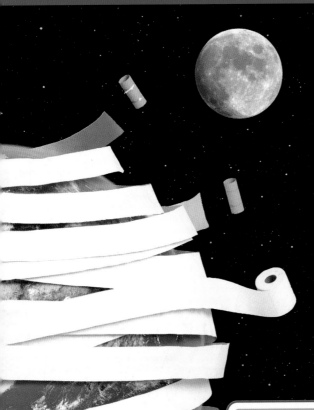

FAST FACTS

Every day, the world uses about 270,000 trees' worth of toilet paper. Fortunately, nearly all of it comes from recycled paper or sustainable pulpwood plantations—trees grown for making paper.

In one year, the average toilet paper user gets through 28 rolls. The total length of 28 toilet paper rolls is about twice the height of the Eiffel Tower in France.

FATBERGS

Toilet paper is made of weak paper fibers that separate when wet, helping it break down. Wet wipes, in contrast, are made with plastic fibers that don't break down. They build up with cooking fat in sewers, forming fatbergs that have to be dug out. Heavy rain makes sewers overflow, washing wet wipe fibers into rivers and oceans, harming wildlife.

THE WORLD'S LARGEST TOILET ROLL WAS EQUIVALENT TO 95,000 NORMAL ROLLS.

THERE IS A YEARLY CONTEST TO FIND THE BEST WEDDING DRESS MADE FROM TOILET PAPER.

WHERE DOES
POO GO?

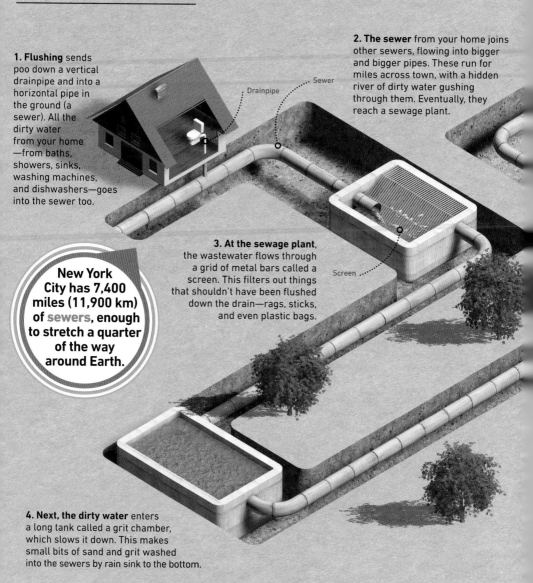

1. Flushing sends poo down a vertical drainpipe and into a horizontal pipe in the ground (a sewer). All the dirty water from your home —from baths, showers, sinks, washing machines, and dishwashers—goes into the sewer too.

2. The sewer from your home joins other sewers, flowing into bigger and bigger pipes. These run for miles across town, with a hidden river of dirty water gushing through them. Eventually, they reach a sewage plant.

Drainpipe

Sewer

New York City has 7,400 miles (11,900 km) of sewers, enough to stretch a quarter of the way around Earth.

3. At the sewage plant, the wastewater flows through a grid of metal bars called a screen. This filters out things that shouldn't have been flushed down the drain—rags, sticks, and even plastic bags.

Screen

4. Next, the dirty water enters a long tank called a grit chamber, which slows it down. This makes small bits of sand and grit washed into the sewers by rain sink to the bottom.

HALF A **MINI COOPER** WAS FOUND IN A LONDON SEWER IN THE UK. NO ONE KNOWS HOW IT GOT THERE.

THE **OLDEST** KNOWN SEWER SYSTEM CAN BE TRACED BACK SOME 6,000 YEARS TO INDIA.

When you flush the toilet, you send your waste on a **long, strange journey** that makes dirty water clean again.

6. Dirty water now flows into an aeration tank, where millions of air bubbles pass through it. Oxygen from the air stimulates the growth of microbes that kill dangerous poo bacteria in the water.

7. A second clarifier tank holds the water for several hours. Microorganisms in the water settle on the bottom, forming more sludge. Some of the water flows back to the aeration tank, supplying fresh microbes. The remaining water, now much clearer, leaves for the next stage.

5. The water is pumped up into the middle of a circular tank called a primary clarifier. Here, it moves so slowly that tiny particles of poo fall to the bottom of the tank and settle as sludge. Rotating scrapers push the sludge into a pit for collection.

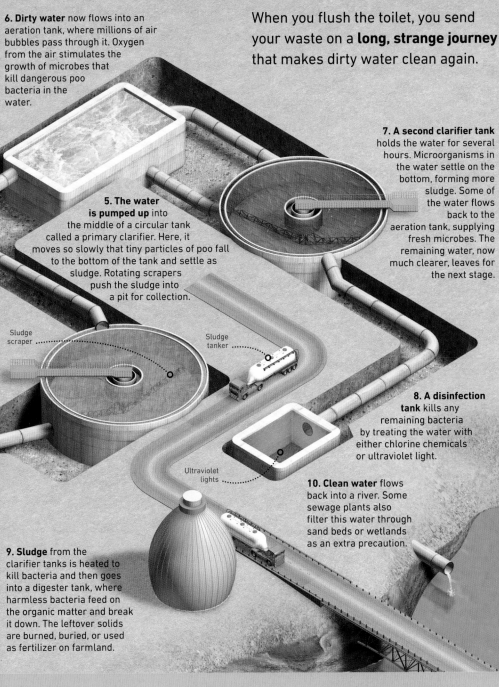

Sludge scraper

Sludge tanker

8. A disinfection tank kills any remaining bacteria by treating the water with either chlorine chemicals or ultraviolet light.

Ultraviolet lights

10. Clean water flows back into a river. Some sewage plants also filter this water through sand beds or wetlands as an extra precaution.

9. Sludge from the clarifier tanks is heated to kill bacteria and then goes into a digester tank, where harmless bacteria feed on the organic matter and break it down. The leftover solids are burned, buried, or used as fertilizer on farmland.

15.5

A 15.5-MILE (25-KM) **SUPER SEWER**, THE THAMES TIDEWAY, IS BEING BUILT UNDER LONDON, ENGLAND.

TWO MILLION **RATS** ARE THOUGHT TO LIVE IN THE SEWERS OF NEW YORK CITY.

HOW MUCH ENERGY
IS IN POO?

The human body has to be regularly **recharged with energy** from food, but our bodies don't extract all the energy from our meals—about **10–15 percent escapes in poo**.

POO POWER

Some sewage plants capture the energy in poo by collecting biogas made by bacteria in sludge tanks. The gas is burned to power electricity generators.

An average poo has about **210 calories** of energy—enough to charge **24 phones**.

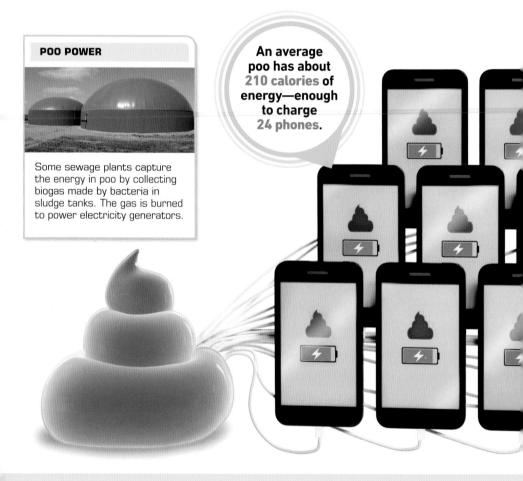

 A DANISH CITY PROVIDES **FRESH WATER** TO ITS RESIDENTS BY USING ENERGY FROM ITS SEWAGE PLANTS.

IN 2021, THE UK'S LARGEST WATER COMPANY CREATED ENOUGH ENERGY FROM WASTE WATER TO COOK **112** MILLION TURKEYS.

FAST FACTS

Every day, the world's population poos out an incredible 10,000 terajoules of energy. That's about as much as 150 World War II atom bombs.

If all the poo in the world were collected and used to make biogas, it could supply enough renewable energy to provide 138 million households with electricity.

An average poo has as many calories of energy as two bananas. If all that energy could be captured, it could charge 24 smartphones or power 45 LED light bulbs for one hour.

A TRIAL "POO" BUS IN BRISTOL, ENGLAND, WAS POWERED BY ENERGY CREATED FROM SEWAGE.

ONE COW CAN PRODUCE ENOUGH POO TO CREATE BIOGAS FOR 1.5 HOURS OF COOKING A DAY.

WASTE
IN SPACE

Rockets are not the only thing **blasting off in space**. When nature calls, **astronauts** on board the International Space Station use special toilets to hoover up **floating feces** and **urine globules**.

Before spacewalks, astronauts adjust their diet to reduce the need to poo inside the spacesuit.

SPACE STATION TOILET

Using the toilet in space can be messy and take up to an hour, including cleaning up. Flushing with water is impossible, so the toilet uses suction to pull waste into it. The yellow funnel is used for pee. To poo, the user must sit very precisely on a hole under the seat while floating weightlessly. Perfect aim is essential.

During a year in space, an astronaut will drink an average 193 gallons (730 liters) of pee and sweat recycled into water.

FARTS ON THE SPACE STATION ARE **SMELLIER** THAN ON EARTH BECAUSE THERE'S NO AIRFLOW.

THE FIRST US **ASTRONAUT** HAD TO PEE IN HIS PANTS BEFORE LIFT-OFF. NO ONE HAD A PLAN FOR PEEING.

Spacewalks (trips outside the space station) can last several hours, so astronauts must wear a special pair of shorts, called a maximum absorbency garment, under the spacesuit. This contains a powdery chemical that can absorb 300 times its own weight in pee.

About 3–4 times a year, space station poo burns up in the atmosphere as a shooting star.

FAST FACTS

The International Space Station recycles urine into water, but poo is stored and later ejected into space.

Toilet

Poo bag The astronaut poos into a plastic bag in the seat. The bag is tied shut and pushed into the storage container under the seat.

Storage When full, storage containers are stowed with other trash in a cargo supply craft attached to the space station.

Destruction Released from the space station, the cargo supply craft burns up as it reenters Earth's atmosphere.

If astronauts ever embark on the long trip to Mars, they may need to find clever ways of recycling their poo.

Fertilizer Poo could be used as a fertilizer to grow plants, providing a source of fresh food.

Space food Another idea is to turn poo into an edible paste, like yeast extract, by growing microbes in it.

Radiation shield Waste bags full of poo could be used to line the walls of spacecraft, creating a protective radiation shield.

THE SECOND MAN ON THE **MOON**, BUZZ ALDRIN, CLAIMS HE WAS THE FIRST TO PEE THERE.

CHEMICALS IN THE SPACE TOILET TURN PEE BRIGHT **PURPLE** AND VERY ACIDIC.

POO
IN THE PAST

Before **flushing toilets and toilet paper** were invented, people found all sorts of inventive ways to **dispose of their deposits**.

In ancient Rome, visitors gathered in public toilets to catch up on gossip or talk business—while they did their business. They sat together on long stone benches with holes over a sewer that washed poo into the river.

Instead of **toilet paper, the Romans used a wet sponge on a stick**, dipped in vinegar.

Toilet

Medieval castles often had toilets that extended from an outer wall, with a seat over a hole so that poo and pee fell straight in the moat. Fashionable ladies sometimes stored their dresses here because the smell kept clothes moths at bay.

English kings employed a "groom of the stool"—a servant whose duties included changing the monarch's underwear, wiping the royal bottom, and cleaning the portable toilet, which was known as a close stool.

Medieval ships didn't have bathrooms. Sailors relieved themselves over the bow (front), either by leaning over the side or by perching over openings in the deck. They used a soggy rope dangling in the water to wipe themselves afterward.

IN 1858, THE STENCH OF HUMAN WASTE IN THE THAMES DROVE POLITICIANS FROM PARLIAMENT.

 BUILT IN THE 6TH CENTURY BC, ROME'S CLOACA MAXIMA IS ONE OF THE OLDEST SEWERS STILL IN USE.

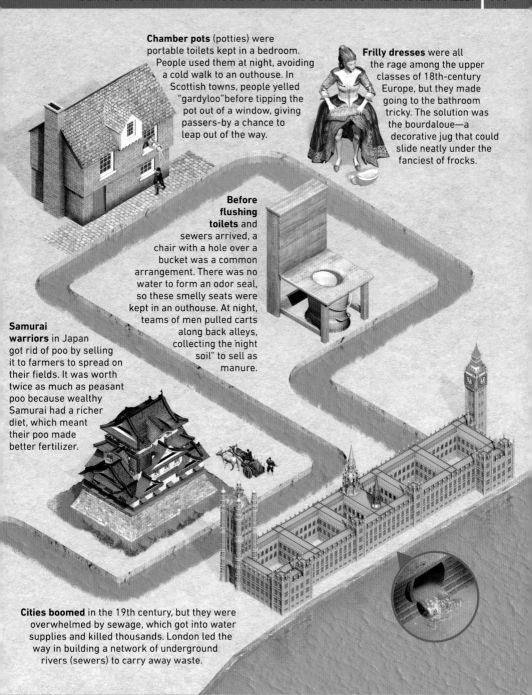

Chamber pots (potties) were portable toilets kept in a bedroom. People used them at night, avoiding a cold walk to an outhouse. In Scottish towns, people yelled "gardyloo" before tipping the pot out of a window, giving passers-by a chance to leap out of the way.

Frilly dresses were all the rage among the upper classes of 18th-century Europe, but they made going to the bathroom tricky. The solution was the bourdaloue—a decorative jug that could slide neatly under the fanciest of frocks.

Before flushing toilets and sewers arrived, a chair with a hole over a bucket was a common arrangement. There was no water to form an odor seal, so these smelly seats were kept in an outhouse. At night, teams of men pulled carts along back alleys, collecting the 'night soil" to sell as manure.

Samurai warriors in Japan got rid of poo by selling it to farmers to spread on their fields. It was worth twice as much as peasant poo because wealthy Samurai had a richer diet, which meant their poo made better fertilizer.

Cities boomed in the 19th century, but they were overwhelmed by sewage, which got into water supplies and killed thousands. London led the way in building a network of underground rivers (sewers) to carry away waste.

IN 1844, NEW YORK PRODUCED ENOUGH HUMAN POO TO FILL ABOUT 53,000 FAMILY CAR **TRUNKS**.

IN MEDIEVAL TIMES, SOME PEOPLE WORE FLOWER-STUFFED **NOSEBAGS** TO MASK SMELLS.

WHOSE
POO?

Leopard
Foul-smelling and sticky. Color varies from pale brown to much darker after a blood-rich meal. May contain fragments of bone, fur, or feathers.

Hippopotamus
Shapeless dollops and splats, very fibrous. Hippos spin their tail like an electric fan when defecating, breaking up the dung into a spray of debris.

Hyena
Brownish when fresh but turning white as it dries, due to large quantities of bone. Hyenas are scavengers and use bone-crushing jaws to devour the remains of carcasses.

Elephant poo is packed with fibrous plant material.

Camel
Very dry, egg-shaped pellets that burn easily. To reduce their need for water, camels have long intestines that extract nearly all the moisture from droppings.

Giraffe
Small, dark pellets, blunt at one end and pointed at the other. They emerge as clumps but scatter on hitting the ground due to the long drop from the point of exit.

Mouse
Tiny dark brown sausages, smaller than rice grains and with pointed ends. Squishy when fresh but brittle when dry.

Black ant
Heaps of tiny, dustlike droppings stored in a special chamber in the nest. Other waste, such as dead ants and food debris, is dumped in a separate heap.

Elephant
Large, moist clods full of straw and half-digested plant matter. Soft and warm when fresh, with a pleasant aroma, but turns hard and crumbly on drying.

OTTER DROPPINGS, OR SPRAINTS, ARE SAID TO SMELL OF JASMINE TEA WITH A HINT OF FISH.

ADELIE PENGUINS EXCRETE PINK POO, A COLOR CAUSED BY THEIR KRILL DIET.

Sausages or pellets? Fragrant or foul? Squishy or firm? **Animal poos** come in an **amazing range** of shapes, sizes, textures, colors, and smells.

Llama
Small, dry pellets, often clumped together. Llamas absorb most of the water from their poo because they live in dry places.

Rhino
Large, roughly cylindrical masses that feel soft and fibrous due to large amounts of plant matter. Often stamped on and kicked apart by the rhino spreading its scent.

Wild boar
Strong-smelling, lumpy sausage made of pellets pressed together in the rectum. Texture varies from fudgelike to fibrous.

Beaver
Packed with wood chips and sawdust, with a rough, fibrous texture. May resemble small coconuts, but oval in shape.

Chimpanzee
Similar to human poo but softer and paler. Strong aroma. May contain undigested seeds, which chimps pick out and eat.

Fox
Small fudgelike sausage, often with a twisted point. Foul, overpowering odor and maddeningly sticky. Color varies from black to brown or gray.

Bird
Irregular splat consisting of a slimy white fluid and darker, semisolid patches.

Goat
Smooth, glossy pellets that exit the body in a sausage-shaped cluster but often break apart and scatter on landing. Similar to sheep droppings.

Guinea pig
Smooth, sausage-shaped pellets, glossy and dark when fresh but turning paler brown as they dry.

Rabbit
Pea-sized pellets that feel soft and fibrous. At night, rabbits produce edible droppings that they eat directly from the anus.

Cow
A runny porridge that forms a flat pancake on hitting the ground. Contains little plant fiber thanks to the cow's efficient digestive system. Crust dries brown but reveals a vibrant greenish interior when broken.

THE TAMBAQUI, A FRESHWATER FISH, EATS FRUIT AND SPREADS THE SEEDS IN ITS POO.

OWLS BRING UP PELLETS OF FOOD THEY CANNOT DIGEST, SUCH AS FUR AND ANIMAL BONES.

Hundreds of Hindus take part in the dung-throwing tradition because the cow is their sacred animal.

MOO POO

Every year people come from far and wide to get dung and dirty at the Gore Habba festival in the Indian village of Gumatapura. Tractors bring in bucketloads of cow dung, and a priest performs a special blessing before the dung-flinging and slinging begins!

WHICH ANIMAL
POOS THE MOST?

The **African elephant** opens its bowels up to **20 times a day**, dumping a grand total of up to 485 lb (220 kg) of dung.

A week's worth of **elephant poo** weighs up to 1.47 tons— as much as **25 people**.

POO PICKERS

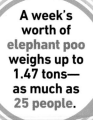

Elephant poo contains lots of undigested leftovers, such as seeds, which other animals pick out to eat. It also contains so much water that some people squeeze it to get a drink.

ELEPHANT DUNG
IS HOME TO LOTS OF
CREATURES, SUCH AS
FROGS, SCORPIONS,
AND MILLIPEDES.

AN ELEPHANT
CAN **HOLD** 7 PINTS
(4 LITERS) OF WATER
IN ITS TRUNK.

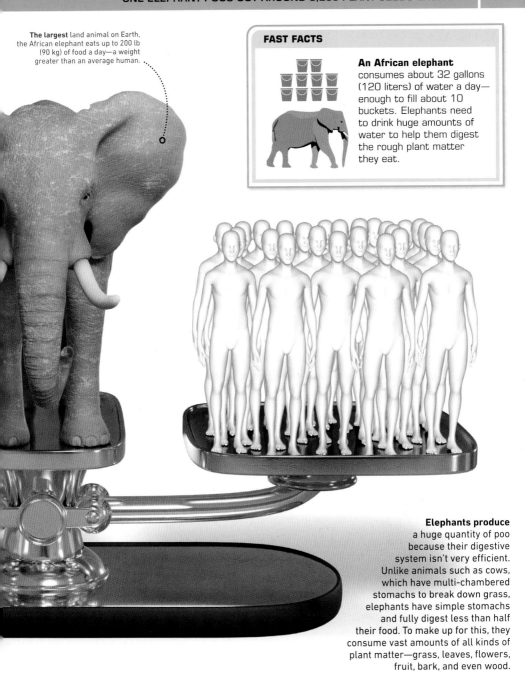

The largest land animal on Earth, the African elephant eats up to 200 lb (90 kg) of food a day—a weight greater than an average human.

FAST FACTS

An African elephant consumes about 32 gallons (120 liters) of water a day—enough to fill about 10 buckets. Elephants need to drink huge amounts of water to help them digest the rough plant matter they eat.

Elephants produce a huge quantity of poo because their digestive system isn't very efficient. Unlike animals such as cows, which have multi-chambered stomachs to break down grass, elephants have simple stomachs and fully digest less than half their food. To make up for this, they consume vast amounts of all kinds of plant matter—grass, leaves, flowers, fruit, bark, and even wood.

IN SOME PARTS OF THE WORLD, PEOPLE SET ELEPHANT DUNG ON FIRE TO DETER MOSQUITOES.

ELEPHANT POO CAN BE DRIED, DYED, AND TURNED INTO BRACELETS AND NECKLACES.

HOW OFTEN DO
ANIMALS POO?

Mayfly
Never
Adult mayflies have no mouths and don't eat.

Snake
From once a day to once a year

Large snakes can survive for more than a year without eating anything. So, there's nothing to poo.

Sloth
Once a week

Sloths save up so much dung between toilet trips that they can lose a third of their body weight when pooing.

Cat
Once a day

Cats are carnivores and produce much less poo than plant eaters. One poo a day is enough.

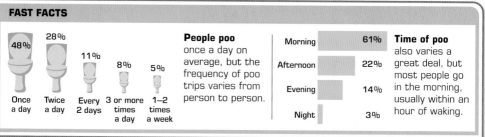

FAST FACTS

48%	28%	11%	8%	5%				
Once a day	Twice a day	Every 2 days	3 or more times a day	1–2 times a week				

People poo once a day on average, but the frequency of poo trips varies from person to person.

Morning	61%
Afternoon	22%
Evening	14%
Night	3%

Time of poo also varies a great deal, but most people go in the morning, usually within an hour of waking.

ZOOKEEPERS HAVE TO CLEAN UP **PANDA POO** AROUND **40** TIMES A DAY.

BADGERS DIG SPECIAL PITS CALLED **LATRINES** AWAY FROM THEIR BURROWS TO POO IN.

Humans poo about once a day, but other members of the animal kingdom visit the bathroom more often or less often than us. **How frequently they go** depends mainly on what they eat.

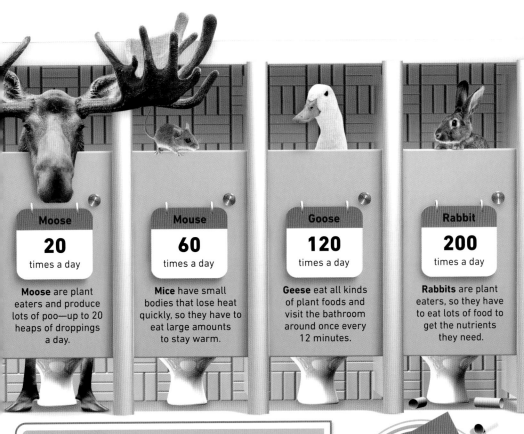

Moose

20

times a day

Moose are plant eaters and produce lots of poo—up to 20 heaps of droppings a day.

Mouse

60

times a day

Mice have small bodies that lose heat quickly, so they have to eat large amounts to stay warm.

Goose

120

times a day

Geese eat all kinds of plant foods and visit the bathroom around once every 12 minutes.

Rabbit

200

times a day

Rabbits are plant eaters, so they have to eat lots of food to get the nutrients they need.

FECAL PLUGS

During their winter hibernation, black bears may have to last seven months without a loo trip. To guard against leaks, their bottoms become blocked by a fecal plug made of dried poo and swallowed hair.

Animals that poo pellets poo the most often—up to 500 times a day.

JELLYFISH DON'T HAVE AN ANUS. THEY **EXCRETE** WASTE, BUT THEY DON'T POO LIKE US.

IN ONE YEAR, **EARTHWORMS** CAN POO 2 FT (60 CM) OF NUTRIENT-RICH SOIL.

POO
PICNIC

Good news: **humans don't have to eat poo!** This is because our diet contains all the **nutrients** we need. However, many animals love nothing more than chowing down on some **fresh feces**—including their own.

The **practice** of eating **poo is known as coprophagy.**

Rabbits and guinea pigs eat special droppings containing partially digested food. The soft pellets, called cecotropes, help them absorb extra protein and vitamins.

About one in six dogs eats poo, but exactly why is a mystery. Wild dogs and wolves eat their pups' poo and lick the pups' bottoms to clean them.

A **CASSOWARY** PICKS OUT AND EATS PARTIALLY DIGESTED CHUNKS OF FRUIT FROM ITS POO.

A 42,000-YEAR-OLD BABY **MAMMOTH** HAS BEEN DISCOVERED WITH ADULT FECES IN ITS BELLY.

The capybara is a giant South American rodent that produces two types of poo: hard pellets, which they discard, and soft ones, which they eat. The soft stuff contains nutrients released by bacteria in the capybara's intestine.

Egyptian vultures get the yellow pigment that colors their face by eating cow dung. This makes them more appealing to mates.

Butterflies get salt by sucking liquid from fresh poo—even human poo!

Baby hippos, koalas, and elephants swallow their mums' poo to get the gut bacteria they need to digest plants.

COPROPHILOUS FUNGI GROWS IN ANIMAL DUNG. THE SPORES ARE EATEN BY HERBIVORES.

IN ANCIENT CHINA, PEOPLE BUILT TOILETS OVER PIGSTIES. PIGS ATE THE WASTE THAT DROPPED DOWN.

Male butterflies **mud-puddle** the most—the minerals help them reproduce.

DUNG DRINKERS

Some butterflies congregate together to indulge in "mud-puddling," which involves sticking their strawlike proboscis into piles of dung before sucking it up. Dung contains vital salt and minerals, which is missing from their usual diet of sweet nectar from flowers.

WHAT USE ARE
POO AND PEE?

Caterpillar poo tea is an expensive Chinese tea brewed from the tiny droppings of caterpillars, mixed with tea leaves. The stewed poo is said to soothe the stomach.

Cow pat–throwing contests are popular in the American town of Beaver, Oklahoma. First prize goes to the person who can fling a dried cow pat the farthest without breaking it.

Gunpowder was once made from the poo and pee of farm animals. When left to ripen for a year or so, this smelly concoction produces the chemical saltpeter. This makes an explosive mix when added to charcoal and sulfur.

Perfect perfumes need earthy or mus undertones—such a the faint odor of poo Perfume makers us synthetic versions o the stinky sulfur chemicals in poo.

Camel pellets come out so dry that they make an ideal fuel for desert campfires. In other parts of the world, people also use buffalo and cow dung for cooking and heating.

RESEARCHERS IN JAPAN HAVE TURNED HUMAN WASTE INTO A TYPE OF STEAK THAT IS SAFE TO EAT.

IT'S SAID THAT ONE EGYPTIAN PHARAOH USED PEE TO HELP CURE HIS EYE INFECTION.

Most of us **flush the toilet** without a backward glance, but not everyone lets their waste go to waste. Since ancient times, people have found all sorts of surprising uses for poo and pee, from **brewing coffee** to **making gunpowder**.

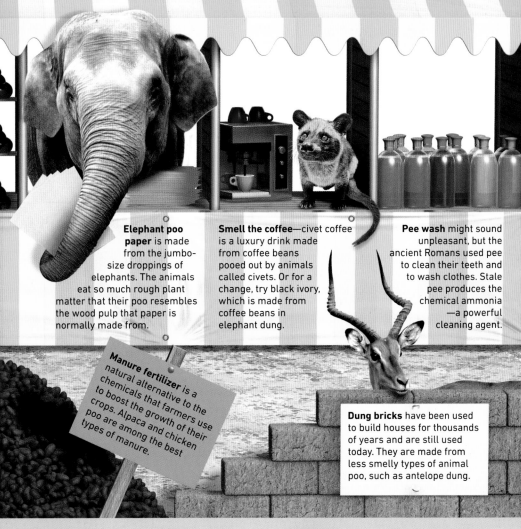

Elephant poo paper is made from the jumbo-size droppings of elephants. The animals eat so much rough plant matter that their poo resembles the wood pulp that paper is normally made from.

Smell the coffee—civet coffee is a luxury drink made from coffee beans pooed out by animals called civets. Or for a change, try black ivory, which is made from coffee beans in elephant dung.

Pee wash might sound unpleasant, but the ancient Romans used pee to clean their teeth and to wash clothes. Stale pee produces the chemical ammonia —a powerful cleaning agent.

Manure fertilizer is a natural alternative to the chemicals that farmers use to boost the growth of their crops. Alpaca and chicken poo are among the best types of manure.

Dung bricks have been used to build houses for thousands of years and are still used today. They are made from less smelly types of animal poo, such as antelope dung.

 **URINE** AND **LIME** CAN BE MIXED TO MAKE BRICKS. WHEN FIRST MADE, THEY HAVE A STRONG PEE SMELL.

 A DESIGNER FROM ISRAEL HAS MADE STOOLS AND LAMP SHADES OUT OF **HORSE DUNG**.

Defensive dung

PLAYING *DEAD*

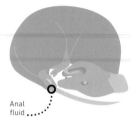

Poo can make a great **defensive weapon**. If a possum meets a predator, its first line of defense is to snarl angrily. If that fails, the possum plays dead. It drops to the ground, lets its tongue hang out, and releases a puddle of foul-smelling, greenish **anal fluid**.

Anal fluid

EGG ESCAPE

Egg

Poo

In Africa's Kalahari desert, trees to nest in are hard to find, so the double-banded courser lays its eggs on the ground. To hide them from nosy animals, it puts them among **antelope droppings**, which are the same size and color.

STINKY SHIELD

The larvae (maggots) of three-lined potato beetles **smear themselves with poo** laced with poison from the plants they eat. This **fecal shield** protects them from birds.

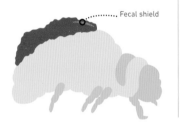

Fecal shield

A TALE OF DEFENSE

Certain South American scorpions escape predators by **shedding their tail.** But this means they also shed their anus, which is at the end of the tail. As a result, they slowly swell up with poo until they **die of constipation**. Even so, they survive long enough to complete their life cycle.

Stinger

Anus

POOP SHOOTERS

Foxes get one in the eye if they bother hoopoe chicks in their nest. When danger threatens, the chicks turn round and shoot a well-aimed **jet of liquid excrement** in the intruder's face. For extra protection, they also smear themselves with an oily secretion that reeks of rotting meat.

Jet of poo

ORB-WEB SPIDERS DECORATE THEIR WEBS TO LOOK LIKE BIRD POO TO KEEP PREDATORS FROM EATING THEM.

IF TOO HOT, **VULTURES** POO ON THEIR LEGS TO HELP COOL THEMSELVES DOWN.

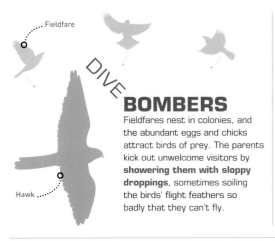

Fieldfare

Hawk

DIVE BOMBERS

Fieldfares nest in colonies, and the abundant eggs and chicks attract birds of prey. The parents kick out unwelcome visitors by **showering them with sloppy droppings**, sometimes soiling the birds' flight feathers so badly that they can't fly.

FATAL FART

The larva of the beaded lacewing uses its back passage not for defense but for attack. It lives in termite nests and stuns its termite prey with **toxic fart gases**. One lacewing fart can **paralyze and kill** up to six termites.

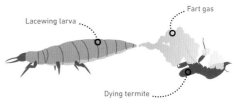

Lacewing larva

Fart gas

Dying termite

SEA OF POO

Whales sometimes resort to fouling the water with a diarrhea-like discharge when danger threatens. For maximum effect, they whip up the cloud of feces with their powerful tails, creating a "**poonado**" that puts off all but the most desperate predators.

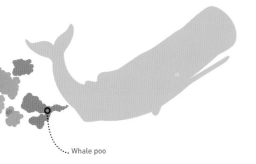

Whale poo

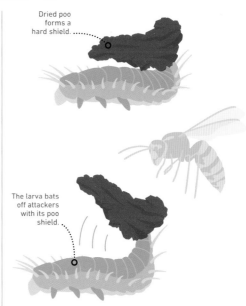

Dried poo forms a hard shield.

The larva bats off attackers with its poo shield.

FAKE FECES

Camouflaged caterpillar

Birds love to eat caterpillars—but not bird poo. The caterpillars of swallowtail butterflies stay safe by **perfectly mimicking** the revolting, slimy shape and colors of a fresh bird dropping oozing down a leaf.

WACKY TAIL

The **telescoping anus** of the tortoise beetle larva is used to dab droppings on the back of its tail, forming a hard shield of **dried poo**. When ants, wasps, or spiders bother the larva, a powerful flick of the tail bats them way.

HONEYBEES FROM VIETNAM SMEAR DUNG AT THE HIVE'S ENTRANCE TO STOP HORNET RAIDS.

BOMBARDIER BEETLES BLAST OUT **TOXIC** LIQUID FROM THEIR ANUS. IT CAN KILL OTHER INSECTS.

HOW STRONG IS
A DUNG BEETLE?

Gram for gram, the **strongest insect on Earth** is the dung beetle. It uses its strength not just to maneuver great balls of dung but also to dig tunnels and fight off rival dung beetles.

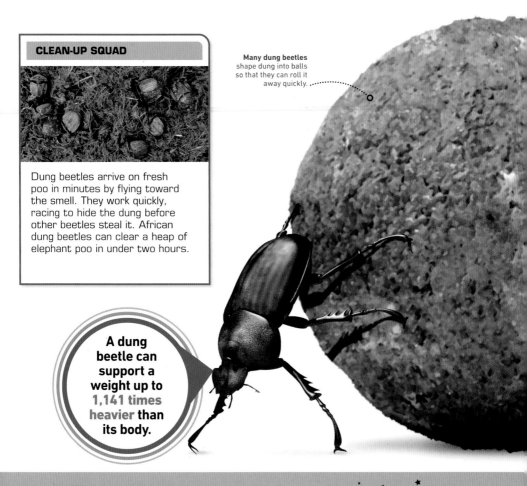

Many dung beetles shape dung into balls so that they can roll it away quickly.

CLEAN-UP SQUAD

Dung beetles arrive on fresh poo in minutes by flying toward the smell. They work quickly, racing to hide the dung before other beetles steal it. African dung beetles can clear a heap of elephant poo in under two hours.

A dung beetle can support a weight up to **1,141 times heavier** than its body.

SOME BURROWING OWLS USE ANIMAL POO TO **ATTRACT** DUNG BEETLES, WHICH THEY THEN EAT.

NOCTURNAL AFRICAN DUNG BEETLES USE THE **STARS** OF THE NIGHT SKY TO **NAVIGATE**.

FAST FACTS

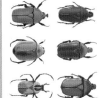

Dung beetles live on every continent except Antarctica, and there are about 10,000 species (types). Most are strong fliers, and many types have beautifully colored wing-cases.

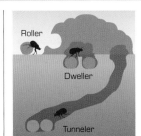

Roller

Dweller

Tunneler

There are three main types of dung beetle.

Rollers make balls of dung, roll them away, and then hide them in a tunnel.

Dwellers make their nests inside a heap of dung.

Tunnelers dig burrows under a pile of dung before hiding the dung inside the burrows.

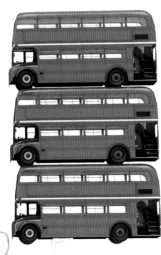

Muscle power
Scientists measured the strength of dung beetles by gluing cotton threads to them and getting them to haul weights over pulleys. The beetles use their muscle power to bury dung balls before laying eggs in them. The adults don't eat poo directly. Instead, they drink the nutritious liquid that oozes out of fresh poo.

If a human could support 1,141 times their own body weight, they'd be able to hold up 78.7 tons—the weight of six double-decker buses.

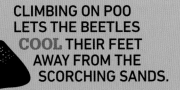

CLIMBING ON POO LETS THE BEETLES **COOL** THEIR FEET AWAY FROM THE SCORCHING SANDS.

FEMALE DUNG BEETLES **BATTLE** TO LAY EGGS ON THE BIGGEST PILE OF DUNG.

WHY IS WOMBAT
POO SQUARE?

Millions of animals make sausage-shaped poo, and millions more produce small round pellets. But there's only **one animal** in the world that **poos cubes: the wombat**.

The square poo of wombats is about the size of dice and is easier to stack than round poo.

Wombats aren't the only animals to mark their territory with smelly substances. Mice continually trickle pee as they run around, leaving a trail of scent marks.

Pottos live in the treetops of African rainforests. They mark the branches that make up their territory by peeing all over their feet and then leaving a trail of stinky footprints.

Wombats produce 80–100 cubic poos a night, usually in small heaps of 6–8.

WOMBATS CAN SPRINT UP TO 25 MPH (40 KMPH) IN BURSTS OF UP TO **90** SECONDS.

COYOTES ALSO USE DUNG TO MARK THEIR TERRITORY AND **COMMUNICATE** WITH OTHER CANINES.

Wombats are marsupials (pouched mammals) and live in Australia. They hide in burrows by day and come out at night to eat grass.

Wombats like to poo in prominent places, such as on logs, rocks, or areas of raised ground. Their droppings serve as territorial markers, telling other wombats that they've visited. Scientists think the poo is square to keep it from rolling away and to make it easier to stack.

PHEROMONES

The pee of certain animals contains chemicals called pheromones, which affect the biology of animals that smell them. The pee of male mouse lemurs, for example, contains pheromones that make other males unable to breed.

32 THE **OLDEST** KNOWN WOMBAT, WAIN, IS **32** YEARS OLD—OVER 100 IN HUMAN YEARS.

A GIANT WOMBAT WEIGHING ABOUT THE SAME AS A RHINOCEROS LIVED DURING THE **ICE AGE.**

WHAT'S THE BIGGEST
PILE OF POO IN
THE WORLD?

Bird and bat poo (guano) can build up in vast piles. A guano mountain known as the **Great Heap** in Peru was 200 ft (60 m) tall, but some piles of bat guano could be even taller.

The Leaning **Tower** of Pisa is 186 ft (56 m) tall.

The
Great Heap
was taller than
Italy's Leaning
Tower of
Pisa.

WEIGHT FOR WEIGHT, **BAT POO** CONTAINS MORE PROTEIN AND NUTRIENTS THAN A **BURGER**.

THE ESTIMATED VALUE OF SEABIRD **GUANO** IS **$1.1 BILLION** (£897 MILLION) ANNUALLY.

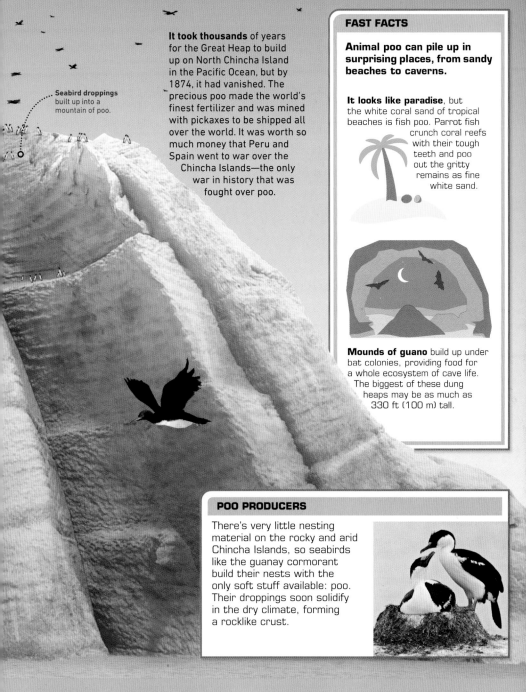

Seabird droppings built up into a mountain of poo.

It took thousands of years for the Great Heap to build up on North Chincha Island in the Pacific Ocean, but by 1874, it had vanished. The precious poo made the world's finest fertilizer and was mined with pickaxes to be shipped all over the world. It was worth so much money that Peru and Spain went to war over the Chincha Islands—the only war in history that was fought over poo.

FAST FACTS

Animal poo can pile up in surprising places, from sandy beaches to caverns.

It looks like paradise, but the white coral sand of tropical beaches is fish poo. Parrot fish crunch coral reefs with their tough teeth and poo out the gritty remains as fine white sand.

Mounds of guano build up under bat colonies, providing food for a whole ecosystem of cave life. The biggest of these dung heaps may be as much as 330 ft (100 m) tall.

POO PRODUCERS

There's very little nesting material on the rocky and arid Chincha Islands, so seabirds like the guanay cormorant build their nests with the only soft stuff available: poo. Their droppings soon solidify in the dry climate, forming a rocklike crust.

CORAL REEFS ACROSS THE WORLD NEED NUTRIENT-RICH POO TO THRIVE.

20 MILLION BATS AT BRACKEN CAVE IN TEXAS PRODUCE 11,000 LB (50,000 KG) OF GUANO A YEAR.

This bat cave houses the largest population of Geoffroy's rousette fruit bats on Earth.

BAT CAVE

An estimated 1.8 million fruit bats fill Monfort Bat Sanctuary on Samal Island in the Philippines. Their cave measures a whopping 245 ft (75 m) long, and they cover three-quarters of the walls and ceiling. People are banned from collecting the piles of poo commonly used in fertilizer to ensure the bats are never disturbed.

Plant-eating animals have a longer digestive system than meat eaters because plants are much harder to digest than meat. Some plant eaters, such as horses, eat lots of food but digest it poorly and poo out piles of half-digested straw. Others, such as cows, digest food slowly and carefully, which requires very long intestines. If a cow's intestines weren't coiled up, its body would be about 160 ft (50 m) long.

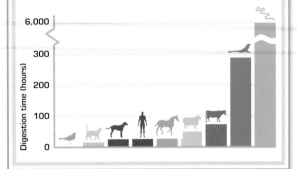

FAST FACTS

How quickly animals can digest food and turn a meal into poo varies a great deal. Food passes through a songbird's body in under an hour, helping it keep its weight down and fly more easily. In contrast, a large snake can take more than a year to fully digest a huge meal after swallowing its victim whole.

A **dog's** digestive system is 15 ft (4.5 m) long—five times longer than its body.

A **lion's** digestive system is 20 ft (6 m) long—three times longer than its body.

A **horse's** digestive system is 69 ft (21 m) long—ten times longer than its body.

A **sheep's** digestive system is 82 ft (25 m) long—19 times longer than its body.

An **elephant's** digestive system is 115 ft (35 m) long—seven times longer than its body.

SOME BIRDS SWALLOW SHARP STONES OR GRIT TO HELP THEM DIGEST FOOD.

STARFISH SPIT OUT THEIR STOMACH TO DIGEST PREY AND THEN, ONCE DONE, PULL IT BACK IN.

HOW FAR DOES
FOOD TRAVEL?

Food goes on a **long journey** as it passes through an animal's body, slowly turning into poo. The trip from mouth to anus goes through the coiled tubes of the **digestive system**, which are packed inside the animal's belly.

The human digestive system is about 26 ft (8 m) long—nearly four times greater than an average adult's height.

A cow's digestive system is **20** times longer than its body.

A cow's digestive system is 164 ft (50 m) long. It takes 3 days for food to pass through.

BAIRD'S BEAKED WHALE HAS A COMPLEX DIGESTIVE SYSTEM WITH UP TO 13 STOMACHS.

HYENAS HAVE JAW MUSCLES THAT CAN **CRUSH** BONES, WHICH ARE THEN DIGESTED IN THEIR STOMACH ACID.

HOW MUCH
METHANE GAS
DO COWS FART?

As they digest food, cows and other farm animals produce the gas methane—one of the most **powerful greenhouse gases** known. Every year, cows release around 53.1 million tons of methane.

The world's cows produce enough methane each year to fill **40 million** hot-air balloons.

FARTING TERMITES

Most of the methane in the atmosphere comes from human activities, but there are natural sources too. Termites fart out up to 20 million tons of methane a year, made by wood-digesting microbes in their gut.

SCIENTISTS ARE LOOKING FOR **METHANE** ON DISTANT PLANETS AS A SIGN OF ALIEN LIFE.

THE AMOUNT OF ATMOSPHERIC METHANE HAS DOUBLED SINCE 1750 DUE TO **HUMAN** ACTIVITY.

FAST FACTS

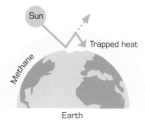

Methane is a greenhouse gas, which means it traps heat in Earth's atmosphere, causing global warming. Methane traps 28 times as much heat as the same amount of carbon dioxide, the best-known greenhouse gas.

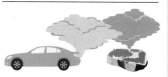

Scientists estimate that producing 2.2 lb (1 kg) of beef does as much damage to Earth's atmosphere (through greenhouse gas emissions) as driving a car for 160 miles (260 km).

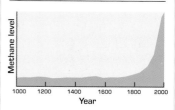

Studies of air bubbles trapped in ancient glaciers reveal that atmospheric methane levels have risen steeply in recent years. The methane comes not just from cattle farming but also from rice farms, rotting landfills, and gas leaks from fossil fuel industries.

Plant-eating animals have methane-producing microorganisms in their stomachs or intestines to help them digest plants. A cow can release up to 630 pints (300 liters) of methane a day. Only a small amount escapes in farts—most is belched out of the mouth.

ADDING SEAWEED TO COWS' DIETS MAY SLASH THEIR METHANE PRODUCTION BY UP TO 82%.

REDUCING METHANE EMISSIONS BY 45% EQUATES TO CLOSING 1,300 COAL-POWERED POWER PLANTS.

Termite mounds can measure more than **39 ft** (12 m) in height.

POO PALACE

Thousands of termites work as a team to build their towering homes. Termites mix their sticky saliva and smelly poo with soil to make these massive mounds. There are tunnels, passageways, rooms, and plenty of air holes to keep the colony cool inside.

WHAT'S THE
BIGGEST FOSSIL POO?

Poo, whether human or animal, doesn't normally last long after it hits the ground, as tiny organisms quickly devour it. However, a few rare dollops last long enough to turn into **fossilized poo—coprolite**.

The longest claimed coprolite is 6 million years old and was found in the remains of a prehistoric swamp in Washington State. Exactly what kind of animal produced this giant poo is a mystery. Some scientists suspect that it might be a cast of a dead animal's intestine. Others think that it might not be a fossil poo at all but just a squiggly mass of clay that oozed out of a rotting log. The record-breaking specimen sold at auction in 2014 for $10,370.

The world's longest claimed coprolite is an **eye-watering 40 in (102 cm)** in length.

GEORGE FRANDSEN HAS A RECORD-BREAKING COLLECTION OF 1,277 FOSSILIZED DINOSAUR POOS.

COPROLITE COMES FROM AN ANCIENT GREEK WORD THAT MEANS "DUNG STONE."

FAST FACTS

The largest coprolite of a meat-eating dinosaur is a 66-million-year-old *Tyrannosaurus* poo, measuring 26.5 in (67.5 cm) long and 6.2 in (15.7 cm) wide. It was found on a ranch in South Dakota in 2019 and was named Barnum, after the paleontologist Barnum Brown.

Fart bubble

The world's oldest farts have been found as bubbles of gas trapped with insects in amber (fossilized tree sap). These bubbles probably erupted after the insects died. Scientists have found fossilized farts of cockroaches, termites, midges, beetles, and ants.

The coprolite was carefully reconstructed from broken fragments.

GIANT SLOTH COPROLITE

Some of the largest collections of coprolites come from caves in the Grand Canyon. About 20,000 years ago, the caves were used as latrines (communal toilets) by prehistoric mammals called giant sloths. Their fossilized dung now forms heaps up to 20 ft (6 m) deep.

COPROLITES WERE FIRST FOUND IN 1824 BY **MARY ANNING**, WHEN SHE NOTICED STRANGELY SHAPED STONES.

DINOSAUR **VOMIT** CONTAINING **FROG BONES** WAS DISCOVERED IN UTAH IN 2018.

WHAT'S THE BIGGEST POO
PARASITE?

Parasites are organisms that live in or on our bodies, feeding on us. The **largest human parasite** is the tapeworm. It can live in our intestines and spreads by laying eggs in poo.

Mature segments drop off the end of the tail and crawl away to escape in poo. If the poo is washed into a river or ocean, fish eat the worm's eggs and become infected.

 **270** TAPEWORM EGGS HAVE BEEN FOUND IN THE FOSSILIZED POO OF A 270-MILLION-YEAR-OLD SHARK.

TAPEWORMS WEAR THEIR STOMACHS ON THE OUTSIDE, ABSORBING NUTRIENTS THROUGH THE SKIN.

A tapeworm can grow to **30 ft (9 m) long** in a person's body.

TAPEWORM HEAD

Many kinds of tapeworms have hooks or suckers on the head so they can anchor themselves firmly to the inside wall of our small intestine. A tapeworm has no eyes, mouth, or stomach. It feeds by absorbing the food that we have already digested.

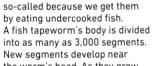

The longest tapeworms of all are fish tapeworms—so-called because we get them by eating undercooked fish. A fish tapeworm's body is divided into as many as 3,000 segments. New segments develop near the worm's head. As they grow, the segments move to the tail and produce eggs. A fish tapeworm can live for 20 years and can produce 1 million eggs per day.

Each segment has male and female parts and can produce thousands of eggs, which are stored inside it.

PARASITES MAY BE THE MOST COMMON OF EARTH'S ORGANISMS, MAKING UP 80% OF ALL LIFE.

MOSQUITOES ARE DREADED, AS THEY HOST A PARASITE THAT CAUSES **MALARIA**.

Record breakers

SMELLIEST POO

Which animal makes the **stinkiest poo**? There are plenty of contenders, from the sickening, fishy poo of whales to the **overpowering stench** of fox poo. But perhaps the smelliest poo—to any animal species— is its own. We find our own poo smellier and more repulsive than animal poo because human poo is more likely to carry germs that can give us diseases.

GOLD FLUSH

The world's **most expensive toilet** is in the showroom of the Hang Fung jewelry store in Hong Kong. Crafted out of **24 carat solid gold**, it's worth about **$2.9 million**. Even the floor and toilet brush are made of gold. But don't think you can pee in style here—the golden throne is never used.

PRICIEST HUMAN POO

Start saving! The **most expensive human poo** is worth **$36,790**. The "Lloyds Bank coprolite" was deposited in York, England, around 1,200 years ago by a Viking who was infested with parasitic worms. It measures a whopping **8 in (20 cm) long**.

FARTHEST FECES

The universe is full of space debris, but not all of it comes from meteorite collisions. Apollo astronauts left a total of **96 fecal bags** on various parts of the moon. They are officially the most distant dumps from planet Earth.

50,000-YEAR-OLD **NEANDERTHAL** POO IS THE OLDEST REPORTED TRACE OF HUMAN FECES.

A BELGIAN MAN SAT ON A TOILET FOR **116 HOURS** IN A BID TO SET A WORLD RECORD.

BIGGEST POO
STAIN

Penguins are the only animals whose poo stains are so big they **are visible from space**. Adélie and emperor penguins live in vast colonies that stain the pure white snow of Antarctica pink or gray with droppings. Scientists use satellite images of the poo stains to figure out how many penguins live in each colony.

FOULEST FARTS

With a few exceptions, such as sloths, all large animals fart. But the trophy for foulest farts should probably go to sea lions, which zookeepers say can clear a crowd of visitors faster than any other animal—thanks to **deadly blasts** that stink of rotten fish and squid.

BEST POOP SHOOTER

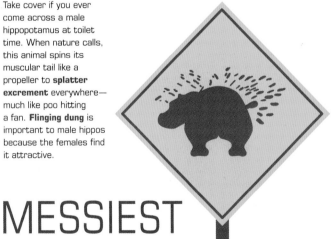

For its size, the skipper butterfly caterpillar of North America can **shoot poo farther** than any other animal. Its ballistic bottom has a kind of latch that holds emerging pellets in place while pressure builds up. Lifting the latch fires droppings 5 ft (1.5 m) away, which is more than **38 times the caterpillar's length**. That's like a human firing a poo across a football field.

Take cover if you ever come across a male hippopotamus at toilet time. When nature calls, this animal spins its muscular tail like a propeller to **splatter excrement** everywhere— much like poo hitting a fan. **Flinging dung** is important to male hippos because the females find it attractive.

MESSIEST POOER

PRICIEST ANIMAL POO

The most highly prized animal poo comes from the sperm whale and sells for **$18,395 per pound**. Called ambergris, this very rare, waxy substance is produced by only a few sperm whales and develops a distinctive smell after floating in the sea for years. It is used to make perfumes smell musky, but some countries now ban it to protect the whales.

COFFEE MADE FROM BEANS PICKED FROM JACU BIRD DUNG SELLS FOR AROUND $445 A POUND.

PHOSPHORUS, A MINERAL, WAS FIRST DISCOVERED IN 1669 IN **HUMAN PEE**.

GLOSSARY

Algae
Simple, plantlike organisms that live in water and make their food by photosynthesis.

Amber
The clear brownish-yellow liquid from ancient pine trees that hardened millions of years ago.

Ambergris
Hard, waxy substance found in the gut of the sperm whale; highly valued in the perfume trade in the past.

Anus
The end of the digestive system, through which feces are expelled from the body.

Archaea
Single-celled microorganisms.

Archaeologist
A person who studies graves, tools, and other objects to learn about people of the past.

Bacteria
Microscopic, single-celled organisms that make up one of the main kingdoms of life on Earth.

Bacteriophages
Viruses that attack bacteria.

Bioluminescence
The production and emission of light by living organisms.

Bladder
The organ that collects and stores urine.

Bowels
Another word for intestines. These organs take nutrients from food for the body to use and get rid of waste.

Camouflaged
Colored, patterned, or shaped to match the surroundings.

Carnivore
A meat-eating animal or plant.

Cell
A tiny unit of living matter. Cells are the building blocks of all living things.

Cilia
Hairlike structures on some cells that sweep substances, such as mucus, along.

Coprolite
Fossilized poo.

Coprophagy
The practice of eating poo.

Digestion
The process of digesting (breaking down) food.

Dung
The natural waste of animals.

Dung midden
Pile of dung that mammals such as rhinos return to and build up.

Embryo
An early stage in the development of an animal or plant.

Enzyme
A substance that organisms produce to speed up particular chemical reactions.

Esophagus
A long tube connecting your mouth to your stomach.

Excretion
The removal of the body's internal waste matter by natural processes, such as urination and sweating.

Feces
Solid waste or droppings that pass out of animals.

Fiber (dietary)
The part of food that is not broken down in the human body. It helps keep the digestive system working properly.

Fossil
The remains or impression of a prehistoric plant or animal.

Fossilization
The process by which plants or animals turn into fossils.

Fruiting body
The part of a fungus that grows above the ground.

Fungus
A type of living organism that is neither a plant nor an animal and feeds off rotting matter.

Gland
An organ in an animal's body, such as the salivary gland, that makes and releases a particular substance.

Guano
Bird, bat, and seal droppings.

Hormone
A chemical messenger produced by organisms to control certain life processes.

Intestines
The tubes inside the body that digest and absorb food and water.

Kidneys
These organs filter blood to remove urea and other waste products.

Larva
The early stage in the life cycle of an animal that undergoes metamorphosis to change into an adult.

Leaf litter
Dead plant material found on the ground.

Metamorphosis
A major change or changes in an animal's body shape during its life cycle.

Microbiome
An ecosystem of organisms living in and on your body.

Microorganism
An organism too small to be seen with the naked eye, such as a bacterium.

Molecule
A tiny particle of matter made up of smaller particles joined together.

Mollusk
A soft-bodied animal, such as a snail or sea hare, that is often protected by a hard shell.

Mucus
A thick, slippery fluid. It is produced in the mouth, nose, throat, and intestines.

Neurological
Relating to the nervous system, or brain and nerves, of an animal.

Non-Newtonian fluid
A substance that can behave like a liquid and a solid, depending on the pressure applied to it.

Organism
An individual member of a biological species.

Parasite
An organism that lives on or inside another organism and feeds from it for an extended period.

Photosynthesis
The process by which plants use sunlight, water, and carbon dioxide to make food.

Pigment
A chemical that gives an object color.

Pore
Tiny holes in the skin through which sweat passes.

Predator
An animal that hunts other animals for food.

Prey
An animal that is hunted as food by other animals.

Protist
An organism that usually consists of a single cell and is not an animal or plant.

Pupa
The resting stage in the life cycle of an insect that undergoes metamorphosis.

Sap
A runny fluid that is carried around plants to provide nourishment.

Secretion
A substance produced and secreted (released) by a cell, gland, or organ.

Sewer
Underground pipes that take used water, poo, and rainwater away from buildings and to the sewage plant.

Spore
A microscopic package of cells produced by a fungus or plant that can grow into a new individual.

Stagnant
A word for a body of water that does not move or flow and can become dirty and foul-smelling.

Toxin
A poisonous substance produced by organisms that can cause diseases.

Urea
The main waste chemical in urine, made from the breakdown of proteins.

Urine
A liquid produced by the kidneys that contains wastes, surplus water, and salts removed from the blood.

Virus
A tiny agent that can infect animals, plants, and bacteria and cause illness.

White blood cell
A type of blood cell found in animals that protects the body from infection and disease.

INDEX

ACKNOWLEDGMENTS

Dorling Kindersley would like to thank the following people for their help with making the book: For scientific consultation, Roberto Berardi of the European Tissue Symposium; Professor Kathie Hodge; Dr. Adrian P. Hunt; Dr. Jody MacLeod, Mainstone Veterinary Clinic; Professor Ron Milo and Ron Sender at the Weizmann Institute, Israel; Savetheelephants.org; and Julian Whitehead. The publisher would also like to thank Katie John and Scarlett O'Hara for proofreading; Helen Peters for indexing; Jacqui Swan for design help; and Tom Bailey, Zaina Budaly, Abigail Ellis, Ben Morgan, and Katie Varney for editorial assistance.

The Original Super Glue® is a Registered Trademark of the Original Super Glue Corporation.

The publisher would like to thank the following for their kind permission to reproduce their photographs:

(Key: a-above; b-below/bottom; c-center; f-far; l-left; r-right; t-top)

3 Alamy Stock Photo: Nature Picture Library / Ingo Arndt (tl). **4 Dreamstime.com:** Lucaar (tl). **6-7 Alamy Stock Photo:** Nature Picture Library / Ingo Arndt. **12 Alamy Stock Photo:** Nature Picture Library / Ingo Arndt (clb). **14 Getty Images:** AFP / Robyn Beck (clb). **16 naturepl.com:** Tui De Roy (l). **16-17 naturepl.com:** Konrad Wothe (cb). **17 Getty Images:** Begoa Tortosa / EyeEm (crb). **naturepl.com:** Will Burrard-Lucas. **18-19 Getty Images / iStock:** Tanto Yensen. **20 Alamy Stock Photo:** Charles Stirling (Diving) (tl). **22 Alamy Stock Photo:** Gaertner (clb). **25 Alamy Stock Photo:** Matej Halouska (clb). **27 Getty Images:** AFP / Daniel Leal (clb). **28-29 Shutterstock.com:** ABACA. **30 Alamy Stock Photo:** Avalon.red / Stephen Dalton (clb). **32-33 Getty Images:** Moment / Picture by Tambako the Jaguar. **35 Alamy Stock Photo:** Paul.Biggins (crb). **37 Alamy Stock Photo:** Itsik Marom (tl). **39 Alamy Stock Photo:** Nature Picture Library / Bruce Davidson (tr). **42-43 Getty Images:** Moment Open (cla). **44 Science Photo Library:** Alexander Semenov (cl). **47 Alamy Stock Photo:** Jack Barr (c); imageBROKER / Georg Stelzner (tl). **48 NASA:** JPL / University of Arizona (tc). **48-49 G. Brad Lewis. 50-51 Mark Lincoln. 51 Alamy Stock Photo:** Historic Collection

(crb). **52-53 Getty Images:** Kyodo News. **56 Alamy Stock Photo:** Vladimir Gjorgiev (tc). **58 Alamy Stock Photo:** Max Allen (clb). **60-61 Alamy Stock Photo:** Imaginechina-Tuchong. **60 naturepl. com:** Eric Baccega (clb). **63 Alamy Stock Photo:** Science Photo Library (tl). **64 Alamy Stock Photo:** Marc Bruxelle RF (cb). **65 Alamy Stock Photo:** Dmitry Gool. **68-69 Alamy Stock Photo:** Spring Images. **71 Dreamstime.com:** Chi Keung Chan / Waterfallbay (cb). **72 Science Photo Library:** Steve Gschmeissner (tl). **74-75 Getty Images:** Cavan Images. **78 Alamy Stock Photo:** NASA Image Collection (cla). **78-79 Alamy Stock Photo:** Cavan Images / David McLain / Aurora Photos. **80-81 Dreamstime.com:** Lucaar. **83 Science Photo Library:** Gastrolab (tc); David Musher (cb). **85 Science Photo Library:** Steve Gschmeissner (crb); SCIMAT (tr, cra). **86 Science Photo Library:** Biozentrum, University Of Basel (clb). **88-89 Alamy Stock Photo:** Cultura Creative Ltd / Callista Images. **95 Alamy Stock Photo:** Science History Images / Medical Body Scans (tr). **96-97 Alamy Stock Photo:** Dennis MacDonald. **96 Alamy Stock Photo:** Rick & Nora Bowers (clb). **99 Getty Images / iStock:** Enrico Pescantini (cb). **103 Getty Images:** AFP / Adrian Dennis (cb). **106 Alamy Stock Photo:** imageBROKER / Michael Dietrich (cl). **108 Alamy Stock Photo:** NG Images (clb). **114-115 Getty Images:** AFP / Manjunath Kiran. **116 Shutterstock.com:** Joost Adriaanse (clb). **118 123RF. com:** Aleksandar Kitanovic (cl). **Alamy Stock Photo:** Rosanne Tackaberry (ca). **119 Dreamstime.com:** Crystal Craig / Crystalcraig (clb); Janazak (cla). **122-123 Alamy Stock Photo:** Friedrich von Hrsten (cb). **124 Alamy Stock Photo:** Paul Riccardi (crb). **Dorling Kindersley:** Frank Greenaway / Natural History Museum, London (ca/moth); Jerry Young (clb). **125 Alamy Stock Photo:** National Geographic Image Collection / Joel Sartore (ca). **Dreamstime.com:** Anankkml (crb). **128 Alamy Stock Photo:** Images of Africa Photobank / David Keith Jones (cl). **131 Alamy Stock Photo:** Ch'ien Lee / Minden Pictures (crb). **133 Alamy Stock Photo:** E.J. Peiker / BIA / Minden Pictures (crb). **134-135 Alamy Stock Photo:** Hendra Su. **138 123RF.com:** Mr.Smith Chetanachan (cb). **140-141 Alamy Stock Photo:** Ingo Arndt / Minden Pictures. **143 Smithsonian National Museum of Natural History, Department of Paleobiology:** Photo courtesy Chip Clark (crb). **145 Alamy Stock Photo:** Science Photo Library / Juan Gaertner (cr).

All other images © **Dorling Kindersley**